MW01421328

PREACHING THE TEN COMMANDMENTS

Timeless Truths for Modern Living

Jeffrey A. Ingraham

WESTBOW PRESS®
A DIVISION OF THOMAS NELSON
& ZONDERVAN

Copyright © 2017 Jeffrey A. Ingraham.
Author Photo © Shané Gilzene, 2016

All rights reserved. No part of this book may be used or reproduced by any means, graphic, electronic, or mechanical, including photocopying, recording, taping or by any information storage retrieval system without the written permission of the author except in the case of brief quotations embodied in critical articles and reviews.

This book is a work of non-fiction. Unless otherwise noted, the author and the publisher make no explicit guarantees as to the accuracy of the information contained in this book and in some cases, names of people and places have been altered to protect their privacy.

Scripture taken from the King James Version of the Bible.

Scripture taken from the New King James Version®. Copyright © 1982 by Thomas Nelson. Used by permission. All rights reserved.

Scripture taken from the American Standard Version of the Bible.

WestBow Press books may be ordered through booksellers or by contacting:

WestBow Press
A Division of Thomas Nelson & Zondervan
1663 Liberty Drive
Bloomington, IN 47403
www.westbowpress.com
1 (866) 928-1240

Because of the dynamic nature of the Internet, any web addresses or links contained in this book may have changed since publication and may no longer be valid. The views expressed in this work are solely those of the author and do not necessarily reflect the views of the publisher, and the publisher hereby disclaims any responsibility for them.

Any people depicted in stock imagery provided by Thinkstock are models, and such images are being used for illustrative purposes only. Certain stock imagery © Thinkstock.

ISBN: 978-1-9736-0208-8 (sc)
ISBN: 978-1-9736-0209-5 (hc)
ISBN: 978-1-9736-0207-1 (e)

Library of Congress Control Number: 2017914033

BMI
Printed in USA

WestBow Press rev. date: 12/1/2017

To my beloved wife, Cynthia. In sickness and in health (Immanuel Baptist Church, New Haven, Connecticut, August 13, 1988).

CONTENTS

Preface ix
Acknowledgments xi

Chapter 1   Introduction 1
Chapter 2   Commandment #1: "Make God First" 8
Chapter 3   Commandment #2: "True Worship for the
            True God" 15
Chapter 4   Commandment #3: "Watch What You Say" 23
Chapter 5   Commandment #4: "Give God His Day" 30
Chapter 6   Commandment #5: "The Ultimate Act of
            Gratitude: Honor to Parents" 37
Chapter 7   Commandment #6: "Value Your Life;
            Don't Take Another's" 44
Chapter 8   Commandment #7: "Keeping the Marriage
            Undefiled" 52
Chapter 9   Commandment #8: "Stop, Thief" 60
Chapter 10 Commandment #9: "Speak the Truth, the
            Whole Truth, and Nothing but the Truth" 67
Chapter 11 Commandment #10: "Give Me More" 74

A Final Word 83
Notes 85
Bibliography 87

PREFACE

This book is the product of a sermon series delivered at the Calvary Baptist Church, Norwalk, Connecticut, during the winter of 2014. The inspiration for the book came about as a result of my teaching the subject matter in our Thursday afternoon Bible study a couple years earlier.

My intent at first was never publication, but simply to introduce to believers a subject matter of extreme importance that is only skirted over in the church. Hence the style of this book is more oral in its structure. The absence of some source citations accounts for my initial objective in this project being nothing more than a preaching series.

While my immediate context and audience was primarily the African-American Church, my desire is that the entire Body of Christ and all readers will be blessed by this book. My prayer for all humanity is that we be governed by the laws of God, and that all come to Salvation by belief in the Son of God, Jesus Christ.

ACKNOWLEDGMENTS

I am indebted to the members of the Calvary Baptist Church, Norwalk, Connecticut for the privilege of serving as their under shepherd for the past quarter century plus. In this capacity my own spirituality has flourished as I have engaged in a ministry of preaching and teaching with them. My preparation in both of these disciplines has allowed me to grow in grace and in the knowledge of Jesus Christ.

In the winter of 2014 I was led by the Holy Spirit to begin the new year offering a sermon series on the Ten Commandments. I had actually taught a course on same about a year earlier with our Thursday Afternoon Bible Study Class. Thus much of my research was already done.

It is always a challenge preaching Old Testament texts to Christians. Part of my challenge was to present new ways of understanding and applying the Ten Commandments for our daily living. The response of our members was very encouraging as they shared with me how they benefitted from the series. This was the encouragement that prompted the publication of this book.

I single out for honorable mention the three leaders of our congregation, without whose co-operation my leadership would be sorely lacking; Deacon John R. Dupree, Chairman of our Board of Deacons; Deaconess Vernell Brandon, President of our

Board of Deaconess; and Mr. Ulysses Whitby, Chairman of our Board of Trustees.

Lastly, acknowledgement is made of the invaluable service of my Administrative Assistant, Mrs. Rosalee Terry. She has served in this capacity for all but a handful of years during my tenure. I applaud her commitment to myself and our congregation. She is responsible for the production of the draft of the manuscript for this book. I marvel at her ability to successfully juggle family life and church life. To God be the glory.

CHAPTER 1

INTRODUCTION
"AN OLD BUT RELEVANT WORD"

In recent years we have seen the escalation of a kind of religious war in America. Thankfully, it has not resulted in bloodshed and the loss of life as we see so frequently in other countries. The war of which I speak is the effort to distance the United States of America from its Judeo-Christian beginnings despite the abundance of evidence contained in the writings of the Founding Fathers. History shows that those who founded this great nation were guided by the truths of the Bible.

The band of English settlers who came ashore on the *Mayflower* in Massachusetts in 1620 drafted, for their self-government, a document acknowledging the fact that they had undergone their voyage for the glory of God and the advancement of the Christian faith. The vast majority of the representatives that met in Philadelphia in the summer of 1776 to draft the Declaration of Independence were Christians. In their declaration they spoke of truths that were self-evident, the first being the biblical understanding that all men were created equal. Eleven years later when the Constitution was written, George Washington signed it, specifically labeling the date "in the year of our Lord."

It may surprise you to know that the constitution of each of our fifty states includes a reference to "God," "almighty God," or simply "divine guidance." Now the war being fought today has centered on the Ten Commandments. Activist judges and liberal organizations such as the American Civil Liberties Union and Americans United for Separation of Church and State have succeeded in forcing areas to remove displays of the Ten Commandments from public view. Perhaps the most notable case was that of Roy Moore, Alabama's Supreme Court chief justice, and his fight to keep a two-and-one-half-ton granite monument of the Ten Commandments in the judicial building. What a sad day in American history when workers began removing the monument!

Today it is not uncommon to hear late-night comedians ridicule and make fun of the Ten Commandments. On numerous occasions multimillionaire media mogul Ted Turner has derided the Ten Commandments as being old and obsolete. He has also said that Christians are losers and bozos.

The truth is we need the Ten Commandments more now than we have ever needed them before. The lawlessness of our times necessitates making them a priority once again. People's lack of respect for one another and their inhumanity toward their fellow citizens make the Ten Commandments more necessary now than ever.

Travel back in time with me. For four hundred years, the children of Israel were in bondage in Egypt. It was not always this way. First, they had been welcomed guests in Egypt. Joseph was there first and had risen to prominence because of God's favor in his life. His family members eventually joined him because of famine in their homeland. Unfortunately, in time, a new pharaoh came into office, one who did not know Joseph. Immediately, the status of the children of Israel changed from guests to slaves. They were sentenced to hard labor.

God saw their suffering and raised up a man by the name of Moses, commissioning him to confront Pharaoh with the demand to let God's people go free. Pharaoh's heart was hardened, and he refused, prompting God to inflict a series of plagues upon the Egyptians. Pharaoh still would not relent, forcing God's hand in sending the tenth plague, which brought the death of every firstborn in the land. Finally, with so much weeping and wailing because of death in his land, Pharaoh relented and let the people of Israel go free.

Now Israel did not experience this final plague as they had been instructed to smear the blood of a lamb without blemish over their doorposts. Then when the angel of death visited the land of Egypt, he saw the blood and passed over the houses of the children of Israel.

During their departure God parted the waters of the Red Sea, allowing them to cross over on dry land. When the pursuing Egyptian army followed them, they drowned. At last, the freed people arrived in the wilderness of Sinai and camped in front of a mountain. The giant mountain began to shake as if from an earthquake as God descended in fire upon it. Such an awesome display of power caused the people to tremble in fear. God warned them that anyone who attempted to come up the mountain would die instantly. Even still, out of the abundance of his grace and mercy, he commanded Moses and Aaron, Moses's brother, to ascend the mountain.

As God had done in the past with the patriarchs, he again enacted a covenant with the people, reminding them how he had brought about their deliverance. Then God gave his chosen people the Ten Commandments, transmitting them through Moses on two tablets of stone. The people wholeheartedly agreed to obey, recognizing God as their ruler.

Then as an emerging nation, Israel needed laws to govern them. Having first been delivered from Egypt, a country filled with idols, the people were preparing to enter their Promised Land. It was a good land, flowing with milk and honey, which God had said he would give to them. Now this land was occupied by other inhabitants, and Israel was commanded to conquer them and take possession of the land. The people there were idol worshippers, and unless conquered, they had the potential to corrupt God's people.

Thus, on the verge of the conquest of this land, Israel needed a national constitution (i.e., the Ten Commandments) to direct them. They needed to reestablish their relationship with the one true God and again become obedient to him. The commandments given on that occasion were representative of all moral, ceremonial, and civil laws found throughout the Bible's books of Exodus, Leviticus, and Deuteronomy.

In the first instance in this introductory message, consider the Ten Commandments' requirement of obedience. God gave these commandments first to his chosen people and then, by extension, to every believer and in fact to all human beings. We must be careful to understand that these commandments are not suggestions or recommendations; they are expectations that God holds of all of us. As our Creator, he expects obedience. As believers who acknowledge God to be our heavenly Father, we are to respond to his goodness given to us by obeying his commands.

As our loving Father, God would never ask of us anything that was destructive or detrimental to us. The apostle John, acknowledged as the beloved disciple of Jesus, wrote, "For this is the love of God, that we keep his commandments: and his commandments are not grievous" (1 John 5:3 ASV).

Thus, the Ten Commandments are meant to guide us in the right paths. Even so, we must acknowledge the reality of our times as being evil and godless. We can use terms such as "moral relativism," the belief that there are no moral absolutes, to characterize these times. Like Israel during the period of the judges, "everyone is doing what seems right in their own eyes!" Thus, we continue to see the deterioration of society as sin and evil run rampant—the sin and evil of illegal drugs, alcohol abuse, violence, and immorality. And the list goes on and on.

God says to us, "Obey my commands, and these evils will cease to be, as now, people will begin to respect, honor, and love each other." Thus, many the commandments are expressed as prohibitions, warning us what not to do, lest we suffer terrible consequences. As our Creator, God knows what is best for us. His intent is not to be a *killjoy*. He doesn't want us to bring harm to ourselves by disobeying him and violating his commands. How much safer we would be if only we obeyed his commandments. How better this world would be if only his commandments prevailed.

In the second instance, note the relationships promoted by the Ten Commandments. The commandments are divided into two parts. The first four address our relationship with God, and the final six speak of our relationships with one another. The Ten Commandments give us instructions for developing and deepening these relationships.

Our relationship with God is the one of primary importance. The first commandment calls for us to have no other god but the true and living God. Once we are in a right relationship with him, then our ability to keep the remaining commandments is enhanced. Furthermore, our relationship with God is strengthened as we give priority to worshipping him. Then we make no graven images of him, give priority to his name by not taking it in vain, and grant priority to his day by remembering to keep it holy.

The commandments, when obeyed, not only lead to a right relationship with God but also result in a right relationship with others. Our parental relationship is strengthened as we honor our father and mother. Our social relationships are strengthened as we do not kill and steal. Our marital relationship is strengthened when we don't commit adultery. Our friendships are strengthened when we don't bear false witness against others. Even our neighborly relationships are strengthened when we don't covet what belongs to our neighbors.

Now the people of Israel were given a reason for keeping these commandments. God prefaced the commandments by reminding the people that he was the one who had brought them out of captivity from Egypt. Considering that he also has brought similar deliverance to our lives by freeing us from the bondage of sin and Satan, what better response can we give but that of obedience to his commands?

In the third and final instance, note the results that come from keeping his commandments. Some believe that these commandments are too rigid, unreasonable, and unrealistic. Nothing could be further from the truth. Adherence to these commandments does not deprive us of anything beneficial. Instead, keeping them adds to the quality of our lives. Indeed, they afford us a measure of freedom.

What does this mean? The people who love, worship, and serve God tend to derive a greater sense of fulfillment and satisfaction from their lives. Those who follow God's standards and allow his laws to govern their lives tend not to have any regrets. Those who honor their parents tend not to have any regrets about doing the right thing. Those who do not kill do not have to worry about bringing loss and grief into the lives of others.

Those who do not commit adultery do not have to worry about sexually transmitted diseases or family units being torn apart. Those who do not steal do not have to worry about being caught and being punished or worse. Those who don't bear false witness do not have to worry about the threat of being discovered and exposed. Those who are not covetous do not have to worry about being tempted to live above their means.

So then the commandments bring us satisfaction. They safeguard us from going down paths that lead to destruction. They guard us from the very present things that will defeat and destroy us. These commandments help protect us from the wiles of the devil, from the ways of the world, and even from our very own thinking and doing. Rather than depriving us of anything, they result in a healthy, happy, and holy life.

In conclusion, though people may remove the Ten Commandments from the public arena, you keep them in your life. They may scorn and ridicule the Ten Commandments on late-night television, but you can cherish them in your heart.

They might call them old-fashioned and out of date, but you can regard them as a lamp to your feet and a light to your path. If the truth is told, to obey is better than sacrifice. Obedience touches the heart of God for his people. Obedience prompts the favor of God on his people. Obedience stirs his intervention in the lives of his people, blessing them, protecting them, providing for them, guiding them, opening doors for them, and fighting battles on their behalf.

Go forth, beloved, on the strength of the following testimony:

> Time is filled with swift transition; Naught on earth unmoved can stand.
> Build your hopes on things eternal; Hold to God's unchanging hands. When your journey is completed; If to God you have been true. Fair and bright, the home in glory; your enraptured soul will view.
> Hold to his hands; to God's unchanging hands.
> Hold to his hands; to God's unchanging hands.
> Build your hopes on things eternal; hold to God's unchanging hand.[1]

CHAPTER 2

COMMANDMENT #1: "MAKE GOD FIRST"
(EXODUS 20:1–4, 7–8, 12–17)

Being number one is a preoccupation with a lot of people. In a highly competitive world, many people want to beat others and obtain the number one position. Be it in exams, sports, business, or career, they always look forward to beating their competitors and excelling as winners. Holding this position makes people feel like they're on top of the world. For them it is the final destination beyond which there is nothing more to achieve.

Now some people specifically desire to be number one in the lives of others. They want to be the person of greatest importance in the life of that other. Usually experienced in a love relationship, those people want the others to orientate their entire lives around them. They insist in knowing at all times where the others are. They insist in being consulted whenever the others have to make decisions. Such a mind-set of wanting to be number one in the life of another can produce the emotion of jealousy. The enamored person cannot bear to see the love interest pay attention to anyone else.

Amazingly, the first commandment is about God's desire to be number one in all of our lives. He said through Moses that we are to have no other gods beside him. Soon thereafter, he gave the rationale for such prohibition, stating that he was a jealous God. Unapologetically, God desires to have first place in our lives. He longs for us to submit to him and allow him to sit upon the thrones of our hearts. Because of who he is and what he has done in our lives, he deserves to be number one to us. Truth is that either he alone sits on the thrones of our hearts or someone or something else does. He doesn't want to share this position with anyone else or anything else. Thus, his command to have no other gods besides him.

Consider now in the first instance God's self-disclosure, not only in this first commandment but in all the commandments. The giving of the commandments in Exodus 20 begins in verse 1 with the declaration, "And God spoke ..." In these opening words is a declaration of the fact of God's existence. We have witnessed in the last few years an assault on God and his existence by an array of self-professing scholars. We have seen their books and watched their presentations on television. They have lectured in universities and colleges.

These have included the likes of Richard Dawkins and his book *The God Delusion*, Sam Harris and his book *The End of Faith*, and Christopher Hitchens and his book *God Is Not Great*. The list goes on and on. Added to the list of atheists are the agnostics, those who say God's existence cannot be proven and that it really does not matter. Then there are the humanists, who believe that man determines his own fate, and the secularists, for whom only the physical world here and now matters.

In response to these pundits who choose to ignore what seems to be the irrefutable proof of God's existence, the ancient psalmist loudly spoke, "The fool hath said in his heart, there is no God" (Psalm 14:1 ASV). So the giving of the commandments begins with God's self-disclosure of himself.

Now beyond God's self-disclosure, we see evidence of his existence in the complexity of our universe and planets. For instance, the size of the earth is perfect, allowing it alone to have an atmosphere of the right mixture of gases to sustain plant, animal, and human life. Its positioning in the solar system is perfect. If earth was any closer to the sun, we would burn to death.

If it was any farther away, we would all freeze to death. All of this points to a purposeful Creator, the almighty God. Furthermore, the uniform laws of nature by which the universe operates point to God. He allows for the earth to rotate on its axis while revolving around the sun. He allows for the progression of day and night and for the seasons to pass in their successions.

Add to these the wonders of the human cell and its DNA makeup, a three-billion-lettered program that tells the cells to act in certain ways, giving us our unique characteristics as human beings. God does exist because he pursues us relentlessly, seeking for us to come to him so that he might satisfy the deep yearnings of our hearts. Now we know that the definitive proof of his existence was when the fullness of the times had come the Word became flesh and dwelt among us in the person of Jesus Christ, being Immanuel, God with us!

Consider the second instance in this commandment, his saving work. In preparation to give his people the commandments and after his self-disclosure, he reminded the people that he was the one who brought them out of bondage from Egypt. Not only was God giving them their freedom, but He was bringing them forth to be his people and be with him, their God. He was bringing them forth to be in a relationship with him.

Such is his desire for you and me. He wants us to have a personal relationship with him. Indeed the salvation he has provided for us in the person of Jesus Christ is not just to "fit us for the sky" but to help us become his sons and daughters. The Bible says, "As many as received Him, to them gave He the power to become the sons of God" (John 1:12 ASV).

Thus, we acknowledge God's deliverance of ourselves from the bondage of sin and the domination of Satan. He brought us out of darkness and into the marvelous light. He drew us close to himself when we had been alienated from him.

Now that we are part of His family, we are privileged to be His sons and daughters. As our heavenly Father, he now makes available to us his bountiful blessings, his tender mercies, his unconditional love, his peace that passeth all human understanding, and his joy, which is unspeakable and full of glory. Being his, we have privileged access into his presence. We are able to boldly approach his throne of grace to obtain his mercy and find grace to help in our time of need—all the while knowing that he never slumbers or sleeps.

And so we better understand that we have no other gods before him, he reminds us of what He has already done for us and indeed what he is doing now for us. Right now he assures us of his presence, not to mention the fact that he will never leave us. Right now he assures us of his protection. He will be our shield. Right now he assures us of his power to strengthen us when we are weak. Right now he assures us of his provisions. He supplies for all of our needs according to his riches in glory. Right now he assures us of his goodness, not withholding anything good from those who walk uprightly.

Third and finally, we see in this first commandment God's sanction against putting other gods before him. He has already established his right to do so. He alone is the true God, and he alone has provided for our salvation just as he delivered Israel from Egyptian bondage.

God now is warning us against the worship of idols and false gods. Ironically, some religions are characterized by their having a plurality of gods. The religion of Hinduism, centered mainly in India, has thousands of gods and goddesses, each represented by idols, statutes, and other replicas. Almost anything you can imagine, especially that which exists in nature, is represented by these idols and statutes. There is a god for the moon, a god for the sun, a god for the sea, a god for the tree, and the list goes on and on. Hindus worship these gods that are represented by the idols. They have major festivals devoted to them. They pay homage and reverence to these idols, and they make pilgrimages to them too.

Truth is the worship of idols is strictly forbidden in Scripture as we will see in the second commandment. We are not to make any graven image of God. Such are nothing more than the product of man's hands. Yes, they may have eyes, but they do not see. They may have ears, but they do not hear. They may have feet, but they do not walk. They may have mouths, but they do not speak. In Old Testament times, prophet after prophet spoke about the folly of idol worship, even ridiculing such practice.

Let us understand that a god is not necessarily something we get on our knees before and pay homage to. Martin Luther, one of the leaders of the Protestant Reformation, said, "Whatever you make the most of is your god." Dr. Lehman Strauss, a former professor of Old Testament studies who hosted a national Bible study program on the air, said, "Idolatry is anything that relegates God into the background. Anything that is more important in your life, other than God, is your god."[2]

Thus, the proud man who idolizes himself makes himself a god. The ambitious man who wants the world to take note of him makes ambition his god. The covetous person who craves money and things make a god out of money and things. The glutton who craves food makes eating his god. The immoral person who indiscriminately sleeps around makes sex his god. Even when we love another more than we love God, we make that person our god. God's response is that he wants to be number one in our lives all by himself. Hence, his sanction that we have no other gods.

In conclusion, when we violate God's sanction against having other gods before him, we only deprive ourselves of the blessings God desires to bring to our lives. To follow after idols and to chase after other gods is to live a life of emptiness, missing the spiritual rest and peace of God. It is to live a life of hopelessness, enslaved to sin. It is to live with the consequences of not inheriting the kingdom of God. It is not being given a new name written in the Lamb's Book of Life and not having the assurance of "being absent in the body is to be present with the Lord."

God encourages us to follow after him and make him first

and foremost in our lives. Only then will we experience the love and power of God working on our behalf such that whatever we might go through, "all things work together for good to them that love God and are called according to His purposes" (Romans 8:28 ASV). When God is put first in our lives, only then are we empowered to overcome the world and the temptations of the devil.

Put God first, and receive answers to your prayers. Put God first, and expect to be greatly rewarded by him. How? By having your iniquities forgiven, your diseases healed, your life redeemed from destruction. You will experience loving kindness and tender mercies. Put God first, and your mouth will be satisfied with good things such that your youth is renewed like the eagles.

Put God first in your time, taking the time to worship and serve him. Put God first in your treasures, giving financially to his church for the support of the ministry expenses. Put God first even with your talents. Use whatever gifts and abilities he has blessed you with to further his honor and glory, declaring with the utmost of conviction, "I'm yours, Lord—everything I've got, everything I am, everything I'm not. I'm yours, Lord. Try me now and see if I can be completely yours."

Jeffrey A. Ingraham

Commandment 1: 10 Questions

1. In Romans 1:20, Paul writes that creation and nature evidence the existence of God. What objection do nonreligious people make to such a claim?
2. In this first commandment, God reminds the Israelites of having redeemed them from Egyptian bondage. What *burden* might rest upon Jews as God's chosen people?
3. John 1:12 speaks of our acceptance of Jesus Christ as the means through which we become part of God's family. How might you respond to those who reject this *narrow* belief?
4. What are other bondages that are more debilitating than iron bars?
5. What are other gods who might rival the one and only God?
6. What reason do we have to exclusively worship God?
7. This chapter maintains that when we love another person more than God, we make that person a god. How might such love be manifested?
8. What consequences do we face for violation of this commandment?
9. The first commandment is like the hub of a wheel, and all of the other commandments are spokes. Offer two illustrations of this claim.
10. How did Jesus relate to the Law, including the Ten Commandments?

CHAPTER 3

COMMANDMENT #2: "TRUE WORSHIP FOR THE TRUE GOD"
(EXODUS 20:4)

Many often tell a story about a youngster who claimed to be drawing a picture of God. He was told that what he was doing was impossible because no one knew what God looked like. Being a somewhat precocious child, his response caught his teacher off guard. He said, "Well, they will know what he looks like now once I have finished this drawing."

Truth is the Bible describes God as being Spirit. He does not exist in a tangible, physical body like you and me. In fact, he told Moses that no one could see his face and live. This second commandment comes on the heel of God declaring himself the only true God, and thus, he alone is to be worshipped. Now he defines what true worship is by spelling out what it is not. God now speaks, "You shall not make for yourself any graven image, or any likeness of anything that is in heaven above, or that is in the earth beneath, or that is in the water under the earth."

This second commandment is a prohibition against idolatry. An idol is anything material that takes priority in our lives over God. Understandably, it is human nature to place trust in something you can see and feel rather than in what cannot be seen or touched. Indeed, it is true faith to trust in a God we cannot see with our physical eyes. Idolatry has always been a contention in the lives of the people of God. When Moses was delayed after he had ascended Mt. Sinai to receive the commandments, Aaron led the people in making a golden calf that they worshipped. After entering the Promised Land, the people of God continued to provoke his anger by allowing idolatry to persist, even though they were commanded to destroy all vestiges of idolatry.

Again, we remind ourselves that these Ten Commandments were given first to God's chosen people, Israel, and by extension to you and me. These were given not to deprive us of anything vital, necessary, or beneficial. They were given for our own good to provide us with boundaries and direction. And if we heed these, we will be in good standing both with God and with man.

Consider now how we first have a word of prohibition. The people were not to make any graven image of God. This would have included carved wood or stone or anything cast from molten metal. In and of themselves, there is nothing necessarily evil about the objects. However, when we lift them up as objects of worship, we are giving to the work of our hands the devotion and honor that is due to God alone. The truth is that nothing man can create with his hands is capable of depicting the one and only God.

Consider the contrast between idols and God. For starters, idols are inanimate objects, whereas God is alive. The prophet Isaiah poured scorn on the making of idols. He wrote that a man would take a piece of wood and use part of it to make a fire to warm himself, another piece to make fire to cook his meals, and the remaining wood to make a god. Such a person used his tools to design, measure, cut, and carve that which would be his god—a product of his own hands (Isaiah 44:14–20 KJV). Jeremiah scoffed at idols, which were incapable of movement and fixed to the one place as fast as a scarecrow in a cucumber field (Jeremiah 10:3–5 KJV). Then the psalmist would add, "Their idols are silver and gold; the work of men's hands. They have mouths, but they do not speak; eyes they have, but they do not see; they have ears, but they do not hear; noses they have but they do not smell; they have hands, but they do not handle; feet they have, but they do not walk; nor do they mutter through their throat. Those who make them are like them; so is everyone who trusts in them" (Psalm 115:4–8 KJV).

And so our God is alive. Being alive, he hears us when we pray. He sees what we are going through. Being alive, he loves us, relates to us, and provides us with the blessings of his presence. Our forefathers testified about feeling him in their hands, their feet, and all over them. The psalmist also said of him that he "neither slumbers nor sleeps."

Also consider that God is formless, but idols have been shaped by the hands of man. When Moses went up Mt. Sinai, God communicated to him verbally unseen. He did not make his immediate presence known. Furthermore, idols are unable to depict the omnipotence of God (his all-powerful nature), his omnipresence (present everywhere at the same time), and his omniscience (his knowledge of all things). Bottom line is that the worship of idols should never be substituted for the worship of God.

Remember, idols are not restricted to biblical times. They are part and parcel of our experience today. Some people park their idols in their garage, others at the marina. Some people put their idols in safety deposit boxes. May we always make God our primary focus, our number-one priority, our greatest consideration. Let us worship him and not some substitute. Let us exalt him and magnify him.

Second, from this passage we see not only a word of prohibition but also a word of explanation. God explains why he alone should be worshipped. In verse five God declares himself to be a jealous God, visiting the iniquity of the fathers upon the children unto the third and fourth generation that hate him. God is jealous, but not in the human sense. His is purely evoked. His is not brought on because of some kind of insecurity or lack of self-esteem. God's jealousy for us concerns itself with our well-being.

This word *jealous* shares a Hebrew root word that's frequently translated as jealous. That is the idea being conveyed here. God is jealous for his own, you and I, we who have been created in his image. He wants only that which is best for us. He desires to protect us from the harm that comes from idol worship. His zeal for us prompts him to protect us at any cost. His zeal means that he wants us all for himself. He does not want to share us with any other person or thing, idols included.

Consider then Scripture's teaching regarding the jealousy of God. He is jealous for his holy name. After Moses had first received the Ten Commandments, which were written on two tablets of stones, he descended the mountain only to find the people of Israel engaged in idolatrous worship with the golden calf they had made. In reaction to this violation of God's command, he smashed the two tablets of stones to pieces. Later God invited Moses back up the mountain for a fresh encounter, revealing his glory to Moses as he had never done before. Then he reiterated his command that his people worship no other God but him and that his name was jealous (Exodus 34:12–14 KJV).

In biblical times names were not just identifying labels. They actually captured the essence of who and what that person was. He created us, and he wants us to be in an exclusive relationship only with him. He wants us to be jealous for him as he is for us. He wants to be our primary consideration, our greatest priority, and our number-one passion. Make certain that you accord him such devotion. Don't be tempted to allow your money or material possessions or any other person or thing to take the rightful place of God in your life.

Besides being jealous for his name, God is also jealous for us. He knows our best interests. Time and time again in scripture, we see God intervening on behalf of his people and delivering them from the oppression of their enemies. We see this during the period of Judges when his people would forget who they were and would seek out other gods. God would then allow a foreign enemy to occupy their land and subdue them. Tasting God's punishment, they would cry out to him. He would then relent and raise up a judge, better known as a deliverer, who would free the people from their oppression. Later in the prophecy of Zechariah, he would explain the motivation for his actions, namely that he was exceedingly jealous for Jerusalem and Zion.

God is jealous for those whom he loves, and he takes appropriate action to help them. This is no different from ourselves as we also take action for those whom we love when they are threatened, abused, taken advantage of, or simply wronged. Because of his jealousy for you and me, right now God is planning things that will bring benefits and blessings to our lives—things that will uplift and prosper us beyond anything we can think of or imagine.

Finally, we also see a word of anticipation in this commandment. Beyond the threat of visiting the iniquity of the fathers upon the children unto the third and fourth generation that hate him, in verse six he makes the promise to show mercy to thousands who love him and keep his commandments. What a wonderful alternative to idol worship, which brings wrath and punishment. When we avoid such and instead obey and love God, we receive his mercy. What better blessing we can anticipate than the mercy of God?

Mercy as a quality of God is his love reaching down to us to meet our needs without consideration of any merit we may or may not have. Such mercy on his behalf has resulted in our salvation, our adoption as God's children, and even our calling to do the work of ministry. Such mercy on his behalf has resulted in him not withholding any good thing from us, him answering of our prayers; and even him willingly looking beyond our faults in consideration of our needs.

While we could never merit God's mercy, scripture does teach that his mercy is more frequently manifested toward those who fear or love him and his servants who walk before him with all their hearts. It is manifested toward everyone who confesses and forsakes their sins. It is manifested toward the one who trusts in the Lord, all those who call upon him, and especially his afflicted people.

Such people who receive his mercy have their sins pardoned after they confess and forsake their wrongdoing. Such people receiving his mercy are delivered from sickness, sorrow, and oppressions. He maintains their security as they trust him, and he acts as a defense and refuge in their day of trouble.

Some tell the story of Thomas Chisholm, a Methodist minister born in 1866 in Franklin, Kentucky. He wrote many sacred poems, some which became prominent hymns of the church. He did not particularly have it easy. Later he wrote about his meager income because of his failing health. Yet this did not deter him from recognizing and acknowledging the goodness and unfailing faithfulness of God. One of his songs is titled "Great Is Thy Faithfulness." For the chorus of that song, he wrote, "Morning by morning new mercies I see; all I have needed Thy hand hath provided—Great is they faithfulness, Lord, unto me."[3]

Each morning if you are able to open your eyes, that's because of the mercy of God. If the blood yet runs warm in your veins, that's because of the mercy of God. If you are able to inhale and exhale, if you have the activity of your limbs, if you are blessed with reasonable health in your body, with sanity in your mind, and with peace in your heart, that's because of the mercy of God.

And so in this commandment, which forbids us from making any graven image of God and bowing down to it, we have seen a word of prohibition, telling us what not to do. We have seen a word of explanation, which tells us that God is a jealous God. And we have seen a word of anticipation, revealing that his mercy is promised if we love and obey him.

Thus, it behooves us to avoid the way of idolatry. Why trust idols? Why reverence and adore them? Why worship them? Why pray to that which has ears but does not hear, eyes but does not see, a mouth but does not speak, or hands and feet but does not move? Why not instead direct such passion to the true and living God? This God is the Creator of the heavens and the earth, the giver of every good and perfect gift, and the one who yet preserves and sustains our lives in this world. This is the God whom the ancient psalmist declared "neither slumbers nor sleeps."

Worship this God because of the benefits you will reap. Your iniquities will be forgiven. Your diseases will be healed. Your life will be redeemed from destruction. You will be crowned with loving kindness and tender mercies. Worship this God because he will satisfy your mouth with good things, and your youth will be renewed like the eagles. Worship this God because he is merciful and gracious, slow to anger, and plenteous in mercy. Worship him because he will not always chide. Neither will he keep his anger forever. Worship him because he has not dealt with us after our sins or rewarded us according to our iniquities. Worship him because as a father pities his children, so the Lord pities those who fear him.

When such worship is engaged, when we gather to adore him, singing his praises, seeking his face, meditating upon his Word, enjoying his presence, exalting his name, honoring his accomplishments, something transformative takes place. Sorrows are turned into joy. Doubts are turned into assurances. Obstacles are seen as opportunities. Burdens become a prelude to blessings. Despairs are turned into delights. In worship the weak are strengthened. The troubled are comforted. The angry are soothed. The anxious are assured. In worship a peace is experienced that surpasses all human understanding. In worship a joy is experienced that is unspeakable and full of glory. In worship faith is fortified so that upon command mountains are cast into the sea.

Worship him, not idols. Draw near to him. Sit as his footstool. Enter into his presence. Worship him. Give my God the glory. Give my God the praise. Worship him. Come, let us worship the Lord and give him the praise.

Commandment 2: 10 Questions

1. How is this commandment different from the first one?
2. What is the major deficiency of idols?
3. Give some examples of idols (shape and size, etc.) in scripture.
4. What are things we treat as idols?
5. What particular experience did Israel have that would have exposed the people to idolatry?
6. This commandment does not explicitly prohibit artistry. Cite two examples from scripture that illustrates this truth.
7. What is the inducement or incentive to not engage in idolatry?
8. Considering that idols cannot properly represent God, what other being or entity can?
9. What makes anything qualify as an idol?
10. What abominable sin did Israel commit while Moses was on the mountain receiving the Ten Commandments?

CHAPTER 4

COMMANDMENT #3: "WATCH WHAT YOU SAY"
(EXODUS 20:7)

It is believed that what distinguishes man from the rest of the animal kingdom is his ability to communicate with words, both spoken and written. While there is the belief that the various species of the animal kingdom are able to communicate amongst themselves with sounds and gestures, this in no way rises to the level of man's ability to communicate through language.

It is through words that we are able to communicate our wants, say what is on our hearts, and express our deepest feelings and emotions. Words allow us to interact with others, making it possible to have meaningful relationships with others. Now the irony of spoken words is that once they have been uttered, they cannot be taken back. Yet how many of us wish we could take back certain words we have spoken—thoughtless words, hurtful words, insensitive words, and even negative words? The truth is that the damage is done just as soon as we speak, and after that, the best we can do is apologize in order to try to save face.

As children, we often said, "Sticks and stones may break my bones, but words can never hurt me." I beg to differ. Words can and do hurt. The child who is told by his mother that he is no good just like his father might be scarred for life. That young girl who is tricked into an unplanned pregnancy because some slickster said he loved her is a victim of the power of words. Friendships can come to screeching halts because one friend uses deceptive words to get the upper hand. The list goes on and on.

God was also concerned about the words his chosen people, Israel, might speak. Thus, after declaring himself to be the only true God worthy of worship, God commanded that no graven images of him be created by the hands of man. The people were prohibited from bowing down to or serving such images because their God, the one who freed them from Egyptian bondage, was a jealous God. Now in this third commandment, God prohibited his people—as he now does us—to not take his name in vain.

The Bible takes promises very seriously. God demands full faithfulness of our vows. To take his name in vain is to use it in an empty, frivolous, or insincere way. After all, in biblical times names were not only used to identify people. They represented the essence and character of those persons. In fact, there were a number of names used of God in the Old Testament to reveal the full nature of his being.

There was Elohim, which was used to refer to God as the Creator. Jehovah spoke of his eternal being. Adonai revealed him to be Master, and El Shaddi, the almighty one. Add to these the compound names using the word Jehovah, and you begin to see the awesomeness of God. He is Jehovan-Jireh, the one who supplies our every need. He is Jehovah-Shalom, the God, our peace. He is Jehovah-Rophi, the God who heals our bodies. He is Jehovah-Rohi, the God who is my shepherd.

Thus, God says we are not to take his name in vain. I submit in the first instance that we take his name in vain when we use it irreverently. While we acknowledge God taking on human flesh in time and dwelling in our midst, we must be careful to not be so casual with Him. He is not the "big man" upstairs. He is not your *homey* or your bosom pal. And to this younger generation, he is no one's *dog*! Rather than being flippant with God's name, we should hallow it instead.

His name is sacred, holy, righteous, and pure. His is the name of omnipotence, omnipresence, and omniscience. Thus, his name is not to be taken lightly or ridiculed. His name is not to be used in frivolous ways and misused. Instead at all time his name is to be worshipped, praised, and revered.

I pity those who take God's name in vain. Scripture says that the Lord will not hold them guiltless. That is a warning of punishment, a threat that God will unleash His wrath. We may not know how or when, but we do know that God is not slack concerning his promises. He will do as he says he will in his own time! Thus, using God's name irreverently will stoke his ire and initiate his wrath upon us.

Those of us who love him are privileged to hallow his name by declaring His greatness, declaring his unconditional love for us in spite of our unworthiness, and declaring that while his anger endureth for a moment, his mercy lasts forever. Thus, when it comes to God, watch what you say. Be careful how you address him. Don't be too casual with him that you lose your respect for him.

In the second instance, we use God's name in vain when we use it insincerely. Think of the times when we identify ourselves as the people of God—saved, sanctified and filled with the Holy Ghost. However, our actions sometimes betray the proclamations of our lips, and our manner of acting does not reflect the image of God in which we were created.

Examples of such actions might include not honoring our word. The truth is that for many of us our word is not our bond! In fact, sometimes we resort to outright lying. That is taking God's name in vain if we profess to be of God. Indeed, scripture condemns lying, lifting it up as a vice that God actually hates. It goes against his very nature as truth. Solomon declared in his writings that "a righteous man hateth lying." Paul wrote the saints at Ephesus, telling them that since they had put off the old man and had put on the new man, they were to put away lying and every man was to speak the truth (Ephesians 4:25 KJV). Furthermore, Paul cautioned the saints at Thessalonica to be on guard for the last days when the evil one, Satan himself, would come with power, signs, and lying wonders (2 Thessalonians 2:9 KJV).

So if everyone else is lying you, the believer, speak the truth. If everyone else is justifying their lies by calling them white lies, you engage in a lifestyle of truth and honesty. You emulate God's unchanging character of always maintaining the truth.

We also take God's name in vain when we are poor testimonies of his saving grace and transforming power. While the world may be reluctant to hear the gospel from our lips, people are quick to read the gospel according to how we live! In other words, people tend to view God through the lens of his people. The prophet Ezekiel recounted how God's promises were questioned because disobedient Israel was forced out of the Promised Land (Ezekiel 36:20–23 KJV). Thus, our insincerity invalidates our claim to the name of God. We fail to treat others kindly as God treats us, and we fail to love others unconditionally as God loves us.

Finally, we take the Lord's name in vain when we use it profanely. Thus, this commandment is a prohibition against swearing. The truth is that we are aware of the pervasiveness of profanity in our society. Many years ago we would say that only drunken sailors cursed. Nowadays it seems like almost everyone is doing it!

We see profanity lacing the lyrics of popular rap artists—white and black; young and old, male and female. It is a challenge to find a movie that the entire family can sit down to watch because most of them are laden with profanity. Comedians feel that they can only be successful if their jokes are laden with expletives. The fact of the matter is, however, that profanity and vulgarity have a devastating impact on society, threatening to destroy the civility and decency needed in our language if we are to respect ourselves and one another. It is commonly accepted that those who engage in such language lack confidence and assurance. Cursing is their sad and pathetic way of dealing with their own deficiencies!

Our first president, George Washington, said, "The foolish and wicked practice of profane cursing and swearing is a vice so mean and low that every person of sense and character detests and despises it."[4] And so to show how limited some people are in their vocabulary and their mastery of words, they resort to cursing, evidencing their immaturity, the feebleness of their minds, and the wickedness of their hearts.

It is an especially grave offense when God's name is used as an actual curse word. Contrary to popular usage, his last name is not a four-letter word that begins with letter "D." It is sinful even when we utter the name of our Lord and Savior, Jesus Christ, in a profane way. If you stump your toe, accidentally smash your finger with a hammer, or lose your money in a game of chance and holler, "Jesus Christ," that's taking the Lord's name in vain.

Thus, the language of the believer should always be that of grace and dignity. We should evidence the change God has begun to work in our lives by the manner of our speaking. May we be moved to live lives of holiness such that our words are pure and beautiful, true and lovely. Only then are we not taking the Lord's name in vain.

In conclusion, our challenge and encouragement now is to strive not to take God's name in vain. If by chance you do, rest assured that he would not hold us guiltless. In fact, you will draw his ire and wrath.

Consider instead the great blessings that come from honoring his name. When we honor his name by magnifying it as an act of worship, our faith is renewed. Our inner man is strengthened. Our hearts are revived. Our bowed down heads are lifted. And our trust in God is reignited.

Hence, we ought to magnify his name every chance that we get. How? By singing his praises, by seeking his face, by studying his Word, by exalting him, and by proclaiming him Lord of Lords and King of Kings. Do it now, friends. Magnify his name. Draw near to him. Sit at his footstool. Enter into his Holy of Holies. Eat at his table, and stand in his presence. Only then will you have a peace that passes all human understanding, receive a joy that is unspeakable and full of glory, and begin to feel something that is inexplicable like a fire burning and a prayer wheel turning.

> Blessed be the name of the Lord. Blessed be the name of the Lord.
> Blessed be the name of the Lord, Most High.
> The name of the Lord is a strong tower.
> The righteous run into it, and they are saved.
> Jesus is the name of the Lord. Jesus is the name of the Lord.

Commandment 3: 10 Questions

1. Of the three ways offered that we take God's name in vain, which do you think is the more common, and why?
2. Biblical names symbolized something in the essence of the person. Cite three examples of such names and their symbolism.
3. Is there a symbolic meaning to your name?
4. What are some of the trivial ways we commonly refer to God?
5. Research another religion to see if there is similar teaching prohibiting the *misuse* of their deity's name.
6. Cite a biblical example of the *misuse* of God's name.
7. Of all the Hebrew names used for God, which one most resonates with you?
8. Of what importance is this third commandment to ancient Israel when they were just established as a nation?
9. It is common to see curse words on T-shirts, but the words will replace at least one letter with an asterisk. What do you think about this?
10. How might we safeguard our children from exposure to and acquisition of profanity?

CHAPTER 5

COMMANDMENT #4: "GIVE GOD HIS DAY"
(EXODUS 20:8)

The fourth commandment is the longest of all the commandments. In it God commanded his people to remember the Sabbath day and to keep it holy. God created the universe in six days, and on the seventh day, he rested. Considering his omnipotence, he rested not because he was tired but rather because he wanted to establish a cycle of rest and work for man.

This was especially beneficial to the people of Israel in that they had just been delivered from four hundred years of hard labor in Egypt. Their slave masters were only concerned about Israel's work production. It didn't matter to them that the children of Israel would get tired. And so this fourth commandment, which prohibits work and encourages rest, was seen as a great humanitarian benefit for the people.

While Jesus observed the Sabbath during his earthly ministry, his followers in time would make Sunday their day of rest and worship. This was because of Christ's resurrection from the dead on a Sunday, and believers started referring to that day as the Lord's Day. Hence, the early church began the practice of worshipping on Sundays. It was this day the apostle Paul cautioned believers to "not forsake the assembling of ourselves together, as is the manner of some" (Hebrews 10:25 KJV).

There was a time in America when the Lord's Day, Sunday, was held in great esteem. Back then, the *blue laws* required stores and business to close. The sale of alcohol was also prohibited on Sunday. It is now rare to find any such place in America where stores are closed on Sundays and booze is not for sale!

The truth is that everything takes place on Sundays now. Sports and recreational leagues schedule their games starting early on Sunday mornings. Schools schedule activities on Sundays. Drive through any neighborhood on a Sunday morning, and you will see people mowing their lawns and washing their cars. Others are in their homes, watching television and reading their newspapers. Even many so-called believers are among their numbers!

Today we urgently need to hear and heed the fourth commandment anew. "Remember the Sabbath Day to keep it holy." How then may we as believers fulfill on the Lord's Day the requirements of this commandment?

In the first instance, we should consider cessation and cease doing some things. The commandments says, "Six days shall you labor and do all your work; but the seventh day is the Sabbath of the Lord your God, in it you shall do no work, you nor your son, nor your daughter, nor your male servant, nor your female servant, nor your cattle, nor the stranger who is within your gates" (Exodus 20:9–10 NKJV).

Not only were the people to cease from labor, but even their animals and their servants were exempted from work as well as the strangers in their midst. Now Jesus declared himself to be Lord of the Sabbath. He said that the Sabbath was made for man and not man for the Sabbath. There were times when out of necessity he broke the traditions of Sabbath observance. One time he allowed his disciple to pluck ears of corn on the Sabbath.

Some people have to work on Sundays out of necessity. As a church, our responsibility is to provide other times for worship and fellowship beyond Sundays. Then also these affected saints who must work on Sundays should negotiate equal time off on Sundays so they could join the assembly of the saints on that day.

Let us be careful here. We should also observe in this commandment the exhortation to work. In fact, we are commanded to work for six days. Work is thus ordained by God. Adam was put to work tending the garden of Eden. Paul told the saints at Thessalonica that if they did not work, they should not eat (2 Thessalonians 3:10 KJV). When man fails to be productive in work, he then directs his energies to worthless and destructive activities. Idleness truly becomes the devil's workshop! Thus, we are to labor and toil for six days, taking the seventh day as a day of rest.

Studies show that if we are to be productive, we need time off in order for the body to rest, recover, and recuperate. Even recreation goes a long way in energizing us to greater productivity. That is what God had in mind in establishing this commandment.

So fulfilling this commandment requires cessation at times from labor. Someone may ask, "But won't we miss out on something or come up short in something?" Ask Truett Cathy, the founder and principal owner of the fast-food chain Chick-Fil-A. As a devoted Christian, he did not want to violate this fourth commandment, and so he would not operate his business on Sundays. Operating only six days out of the week, Chick-Fil-A has been more profitable than any other similar fast-food restaurant.

Let us also ask Erick Liddell of "Chariots of Fire" fame. He was a runner from Scotland on his way to fame and fortune, running in the Olympics of 1924. When he discovered that his race had been scheduled on a Sunday, he politely declined even though his teammates urged him to run. In time God honored him because he had honored God. He served God as a missionary in China, allowing many in that communist nation to hear the gospel of God's love for a fallen world.

What about your witness on the Lord's Day? How big of a deal is the Lord's Day with you? Is it any different from other days?

In the second instance, we fulfill the fourth commandment to remember the Sabbath by our engaging in contemplation. When this commandment was given, the people of God, Israel, were to keep that day holy. On that day in particular, they were to focus their minds and hearts on God, reflecting on all he had done on their behalf. Again, at the outset in giving these commandments, He reminded them that he had brought them out of the land of Egypt and out of bondage.

The retelling of the commandments in Deuteronomy 5 sets them all in the context of a covenant, an agreement. Because God had helped with their escape from slavery in Egypt, his commandments were binding upon them. They were never to forget that fact, and they were to be conscious of it at all times. In similar fashion the Lord has also effected a deliverance in our lives that also calls for reflection and contemplation on the Lord's Day.

While we should never forget what the Lord has done for us, we should be especially mindful of such on the Lord's Day. Beyond the salvation of our souls, we have also experienced the blessings expressed by the ancient psalmist in Psalm 103. God has forgiven all our iniquities and redeemed our lives from destruction.

Consider our predicament. We were born in sin and shaped in iniquity. Our sin separated us from God and made us eligible for the death penalty. The Bible declares, "The wages of sin is death," and it also says, "The soul that sinneth shall surely die." But God, motivated by his love for the world, sent his only begotten Son into the world so that "whoever believes in Him shall not perish, but shall have everlasting life" (John 3:16 KJV).

Thus, by the substitutionary death of Jesus on the cross of Calvary, the unmeasured, righteous judgment of God against sinners was met. So on the Lord's Day, we should always remember that Christ's death was the ransom paid for the sinner, thereby freeing us from just condemnation.

Because of such act, we have been saved and reconciled back to God. We have become new creatures in Christ, old things passing away and all things becoming new. So too, we have been given new names written down in glory in the Lamb's Book of Life. Because of Christ's selfless act of dying in our place, we have been spared that place where there is weeping and gnashing of teeth and unending torment. Instead we have the promise "To be absent in the body is to be present with the Lord" (2 Corinthians 5:8 KJV).

So when we gather on the Lord's Day, let us not fail to remember and contemplate all that he has done for us. Had it not been for the Lord on our side, where would we be! I often say, "Oh, oh, oh, oh, what he's done for me. Oh, oh, oh, oh what he's done for me. Oh, oh, oh, oh what he's done for me. I never shall forget what he's done for me."

In the third and final instance, we remember the Sabbath by engaging in celebration. After our cessation and our contemplation, we are led to our celebration on the Lord's Day. Celebration is all about worship.

Worship is our joyful response to the presence and person of the almighty God. Because he is present to us, we can worship him. While he is present everywhere at the same time, his presence is especially felt in his house and particularly on his day. It is here that we sense his presence as in no other place. It is here that he is high and lifted up. It is said that worship for the believer is like breathing for living beings. As breathing is a natural act that we do without really thinking, worship is to be our natural response to God, especially on the Lord's Day in the Lord's house.

Worship is bowing in the presence of God and offering him our prayers, praise, and thanksgiving. It is recognizing his attributes and responding fervently with all of our heart just because he has acted on our behalf and continues to bless us in the present. In worship we express our love for him, singing songs about him, reading and sharing his Word, and offering ourselves in total submission to him.

It is our duty as believers to worship God. He is our holy, wise, and loving heavenly Father. He is seeking true worshippers, not those who have to be forced or enticed to do so. He only wants those who are convicted to do so. These true worshippers recognize the hand of the Lord in their lives. They recognize that they are the recipients of God's loving-kindness and tender mercies. They have received from God good and perfect gifts and now experience him as the sustainer and preserver of their lives.

Our challenge is to worship God in spirit, in truth, and in the very beauty of holiness. That means we put our hearts into worship as we affirm the biblical truths about God. When there is true worship, the Father is satisfied. He has found what he sought. When there is true worship, the worshipper is satisfied. His highest joy has been experienced. The worshipper is transformed into Christlikeness.

Hear the testimony of theologian Karl Barth, "Worship is the most momentous, the most urgent, and the most glorious action that can take place in the human life."[6] Such was the privilege of the ancient psalmist as he invoked the people of God to praise the Lord time and time again. "To enter His gates with thanksgiving in their hearts and to enter His courts with Praise to say this is the day the Lord has made, I will rejoice for He has made me glad" (Psalm 100:4 KJV).

Thus, we are to remember the Sabbath Day and keep it holy. On the Lord's Day, give him the priority of your worship and your praise. On the Lord's Day, "do not forsake the assembling of yourselves together, as is the manner of some" (Hebrews 10:25 KJV). On the Lord's Day, bring to him the offering of yourself. Lay yourself on the altar of sacrifice. On the Lord's Day, bring to him the offering of your finances, recognizing that all you have is a gift from God that you have freely received. In your giving, remember that to whom much is given, much is required.

On the Lord's Day, bring the offering of your testimony. "I really love the Lord. I really love the Lord. You don't know what he's done for me. He gave me the victory. I love him. I love him. I really love the Lord."

Commandment 4: 10 Questions

1. Are you aware of congregations that worship on Saturday?
2. What is their reason for doing so on that day?
3. How do you respond as a believer?
4. Cite some restrictions ancient Israel observed in fulfilling this commandment's prohibition against work on the Sabbath.
5. How do you reconcile believers being encouraged to not work on the Lord's Day with believers who like to *eat out* on the Lord's Day?
6. Is it possible for professions and services such as hospitals, police, and firefighters to fulfill this commandment?
7. Recreation is sometimes considered to be part of the *rest* associated with this commandment. What might be examples of appropriate and inappropriate recreation on the Lord's Day?
8. What is your state or country's statute concerning the sale of alcohol on the Lord's Day? What are your thoughts about this?
9. In the book of Romans, Paul makes the argument that all days are *holy* days. Why is it that other gatherings of the congregation on other days are sparsely attended by believers?
10. How do you reconcile the *work* of the clergy on the Lord's Day with the requirement of *rest*?

CHAPTER 6

COMMANDMENT #5: "THE ULTIMATE ACT OF GRATITUDE: HONOR TO PARENTS"
(EXODUS 20:12)

The family is the first institution established by God on the earth, and it is of vital importance. After God created the first man and the first woman, Adam and Eve, they became husband and wife. Eve then bore a son, thereby forming the first family. Since then, the family has been the foundation and bedrock of civilization. As the family goes, so does society. Indeed, many of the social ills that now plague our communities can be traced back to the deterioration of the family structure. Fix the family, and the result would be a better society.

This fifth commandment shifts our focus from our relationship with God to our relationships with others, beginning with the family. You may recall the first commandment establishing God as the only true God. The second commandment forbids the creation of any man-made object of worship. The third commandment forbids us from disrespecting God by taking his name in vain. The fourth commandment directs God's people to focus on His work of creation. After six days of creating his world, he rested on the seventh day, the Sabbath. Thus, we are to remember that day and keep it holy.

Now before we can have a meaningful relationship with others, we have to learn how to function in our own families.

Thank God for his wisdom in making the family the vehicle through which we enter the world. It is His intent that families serve to support, protect, nurture, and love us throughout our entire lives. Since parents are the exclusive vessels through which we are birthed into the world, it is of the utmost importance that we engage in the ultimate act of gratitude by honoring our parents. How then are we to fulfill the requirement of this fifth commandment?

In the first instance, consider the parental role. Long before children need to honor their parents, parents have roles to play first. They have the responsibility of rearing the child and creating the kind of home environment such that in time their children naturally come to honor them.

My suspicion is that from the time of our first parents, Adam and Eve, parents have discovered that parenting is not an easy job. In fact, it is one filled with challenges. On the one hand, parents may be too strict and rigid, not allowing their children any freedoms at all. Unfortunately, this only produces children who lack confidence and self-esteem. Then there are those parents at the other extreme. They are too liberal, and they don't set any boundaries for their children, allowing them to do whatever they feel like doing. This style of parenting only produces permissive children whose actions are harmful and also bring shame and despair to their families.

Truth is that it is parents and families who have the responsibility of shaping and molding the lives of their children, such that in time they become responsible and contributing adults in society. In most instances, children grow up to become what they observe in their families. Live a life of unrestraint, and see what Junior becomes later in life. Live a life of lying, stealing, and cheating, and chances are Lil Mary will in time do the same. Live a life of laziness and idleness, and your children will have a sense of entitlement that the government is responsible for taking care of you. Chances are your children (to the third and fourth generations) will feel and act likewise.

Conversely, live a life of industry, hard work, dedication, and commitment, and chances are great that your little ones will follow suit in time. Our children will not do so much what we tell them to do, but they will do what they see us doing!

Now beyond such basic necessities as food, shelter, and clothing, the greatest contribution parents can make in the lives of their children is instilling values in them. Parents should strive to be godly in their everyday living. This means that parents should have a relationship with God by their acceptance of his Son, Jesus Christ, as their Lord and Savior. They should cultivate that relationship by their study of his Word, unceasingly going to him in prayer and frequently and fervently worshipping him. Then they should encourage the same in their children, praying with them, worshipping with them, and serving God with them. The installation of such faith in the lives of their children means that when they become old, they will not depart from such training.

Second, beyond the parental role, this commandment includes the child's response. The commandment says that children are to honor their father and mother. In the book of Ephesians, the apostle Paul amplifies this commandment. He writes. "Children, obey your parents in the Lord, for this is right. Honor your father and mother, which is the first commandment with promise" (Ephesians 6:1–2 ASV).

The biblical understanding of obedience is to hear, grasp what is communicated, and act on it. The people of God were required to obey him as a condition of his favor upon them and as an expression of his relationship to them as heavenly Father. If they disobeyed him, they would find only tragedy and have to experience necessary discipline.

God still commands a similar response of children to parents. Note, however, that while their obedience is pleasing to their parents, it is also pleasing to God. At this stage in the relationship between parent and child, the child is still under the parents' authority. Thus, children who have yet to become adults are commanded to obey their parents even when they may not feel like it. They are to obey in spite of other youths they may know who do not obey their parents!

Of course, the greatest example we have of obedience of children to their parents is that of Jesus himself. While obedient to his heavenly Father, he was also obedient to his earthly parents. That contributed to his growth and becoming strong in spirit, filled with wisdom; and the grace of God being upon Him (Luke 2:40 ASV). Thus, dear children, if Jesus could obey his parents, you can too.

In addition to obeying parents, children are to honor them as well. The word *honor* means to hold in high esteem. This is especially so when the children become of age and perhaps become parents too. While acknowledging that no parents are entirely perfect, they should be honored just the same if only because they gave birth to their children. In addition to the almighty God, we owe our very existence to our parents.

Now such honor needs to be earned by the parents. This is done as parents provide for their children; love their children unconditionally, live godly in the presence of their children, and even discipline their children. To honor them is to think well and good of them, to think highly about them, to speak well of them, and to not cause them any undue grief. To honor them particularly in their twilight years is to help take care of them and even provide for them materially and financially as God enables us. Besides the many biblical verses exhorting children to honor their parents, scripture also threatens the penalty of death for those who disrespect their parents (Leviticus 20:9 KJV).

Thank God for one Anna Jarvis (1908) and one Sonora Louise Smart Dodd, the respective founders of Mother's Day and Father's Day. However, we should not wait for these two days to honor our parents. Let us do so every day as God gives us opportunity.

Finally, the fulfillment of this fifth commandment not only involves the parental role and the child's response but also includes a promised reward. The commandment says, "Honor they father and they mother: that they days may be long upon the Land which the Lord, thy God, giveth thee" (Exodus 20:12 KJV).

Now we must be careful not to interpret this in an absolute sense that we will live extraordinarily long because we have honored them! There are many such people who did fulfill this commandment but did not come anywhere near the promised three score years and ten mentioned by the psalmist (Proverbs 90:10 KJV). One way of looking at this commandment is qualitatively, not quantitatively.

In this sense, our lives are enriched when we obey God in honoring our parents. Such an act of dedication, devotion, and care prompts the favor of God in our lives. It makes him delight to hear and answer our prayers, to supply all our needs according to his riches in glory, and to be present to us in our time of trouble, fighting our battles and making our enemies become our footstools.

So then honor your parents and watch the hand of God act on your behalf, strengthening you in your times of weakness, healing you in your time of sickness, giving you hope in your times of despair, and increasing your faith in the midst of your doubt. This God who commands you to honor those who brought you into this world promises you the sufficiency of his grace—his grace to take care of you, to provide for you, to protect you from dangers seen and unseen, and to help you endure the ups and downs, the trials and tribulations, the uncertainty of these times.

Honor your parents then because God demands it. It is the right thing to do. It will add quality to your life. It will bless you. And most of all, God will be pleased with you.

Thank God that he knows what is best for us. Honoring your

parents result in a happy, loving, and peaceful home. Such honor helps to produce godly offspring, obedient kids, and children who love God and who love God's people. These are the kind of people our world needs today, ones who benefit our world, who help to create good communities and neighborhoods, even a better world.

I now bid you farewell as I magnify that one who was the most obedient of all, that one who honored his parents beyond measure, that one who never did anything wrong. He never spoke a word he ever regretted and wished he could take back. He never once caused his parents a moment of grief because of bad behavior.

God honored Jesus because he honored his parents. God made him not just the Savior of the world but the blesser of the world as well. He said that he had come so that we might have life and have it more abundantly. Thus, because of him, we now have hope for every despair, deliverance for every bondage, strength for every weakness, wisdom for every decision, peace in every confusion, and a friend even for the friendless.

Thank God for Jesus, our Savior and our example, our master and our friend, our lily of the valley and our bright and morning star, our rose of Sharon and our light of the world, our church's head as well as our church's foundation.

Thank God for Jesus, the object of our praise and worship, the author of our salvation, the giver of every good and perfect gift, the strength of our days, the pilot of our ships, the delight of our souls, the cause of our hope. What manner of man is he! That's why we love him, trust him, worship him, adore him, honor him, exalt him, and praise him. Every day with Jesus is sweeter than the day before.

Commandment 5: 10 Questions

1. Cite a scripture reference that obligates offspring to provide for their parents.
2. How do you see the family as being the foundation of society?
3. Scripture is clear on the responsibility of parents to provide for their children, including materially. Is it *right* for families to produce children they are unable to provide for in a material sense?
4. What are challenges that offspring face in caring for their aged parents while still honoring them?
5. In 2015, the United States of America joined several other countries in legalizing same-sex marriage. What challenges might this present to offspring from these unions, especially since both nature and scripture only endorse heterosexual marriage?
6. Is it possible to prompt honor from offspring by materialism? What about parents who lack such means?
7. Is there some conduct parents might engage in that makes them forfeit any honor from their offspring?
8. Is honor shown when children address their parents by first names?
9. Is honor possible when parents see their children as friends?
10. What are some practical ways to demonstrate honor for parents?

CHAPTER 7

COMMANDMENT #6: "VALUE YOUR LIFE; DON'T TAKE ANOTHER'S"
(EXODUS 20:13)

In 1972, as a result of the case of *Furman v. Georgia*, capital punishment (the death sentence) was abolished in the United States because the court saw it as arbitrary and capricious. By this, the court meant that there was no rational explanation for why some people received that sentence and others did not for the commission of the same crime of murder. Of course, capital punishment was eventually restored in 1975.

Travel back in time with me for a short while. In the mid-1970s in Chicago, at least thirty-three teenage boys and young men were murdered by John Wayne Gacy. He lured his victims to his home by force or deception and then strangled them to death. His first victim was actually stabbed to death. Most of his victims were buried in the crawl spaces of his home. Gacy received the death sentence and was executed by lethal injection in May 1994.

In Oklahoma City, Oklahoma, on April 19, 1995, Timothy James McVeigh detonated a truck bomb in front of the Alfred P. Murrah Federal Building. The attack killed 168 people and injured more than six hundred. On June 11, 2001, he was executed by the state by lethal injection.

In October 2002, in the Virginia, Maryland, and the Washington Metropolitan areas, John Allen Muhammad and

Lee Boyd Malvo held this region in the grip of fear and terror for twenty three days. From the back seat and trunk of their car, they indiscriminately fired shots at people as they went about their everyday activities. At least ten people were killed in the process. On November 10, 2009, John Allen Muhammad was executed by lethal injection in the state of Virginia.

Of all the commandments, none evokes the kind of passionate response as the sixth commandment, which prohibits killing. In fact, of all the commandments, the violation of this one is final and unchangeable. Once a person has been killed, all the knowledge and technology of the medical profession cannot restore life to the individual. Indeed, of all the experiences we may have in life, none is as final as death!

Yes, we can start honoring our parents if we weren't. We can stop committing adultery and even reestablish a marriage relationship. We can make restitution if we have stolen and begin speaking the truth if we have lied. We can stop coveting what belongs to our neighbor and feel satisfied with what we have. But if you kill another person, violating this sixth commandment, there is no turning back the hands of time. No wonder then the scriptures have much to say about this commandment.

In examining this commandment, we will consider in the first instance the source of life. As we have seen already in the introductory message (chapter 1), God gave these commandments initially to Israel and by extension ourselves. He is the God who "formed man from the dust of the ground and breathed into his nostrils the breath of life; and man became a living soul" (Genesis 2:7 KJV). More specifically, God created man in his own image (Genesis 1:27 KJV).

Thus, we owe our very existence to God. Our very lives are dependent upon God. Even now God sustains and preserves our lives. He makes provisions for us, allowing us the ability to secure the basic necessities of life and sometimes even more. Furthermore, in most instances, even during times when we are not even aware, God protects us from dangers seen and unseen. Indeed, if it were not for him, we never would have made it.

Now since God is the giver and sustainer of life, only he can say when life should end. Any violation of this sixth commandment is to usurp or hijack a right that belongs only to God. Job wrote that our days are determined by God and the number of our months are in his hands (Job 14:5 KJV). While we acknowledge that God uses the agency of human beings to bring life into the world through birth, he is ultimately the cause of such life. Thus, what God has created (that which right fully belongs to him) no one else has the right to take it away.

Ironically, when the fate of the murderer is being determined, more people seem to express sympathy for him or her rather than the murdered victim who was spared no mercy. While the law in many states calls for the death penalty of such cases, murderers oftentimes solicit more sympathy than their now deceased victims.

I recall a few years ago when I participated in a forum about abolishing capital punishment in the state of Connecticut. One audience member from the area who experienced the murder of five family members in a horrific and gruesome attack said she felt the death sentence should be eliminated because it did not serve as a deterrent to murder! I responded by saying that if we took her logic to heart, we might as well remove the speeding laws because people still speed and that we might as well remove the laws regarding theft because people still steal. And the list goes on and on.

The point I was laboring to make was that people do not want to acknowledge the role of punishment for crimes such as murder. Yes, people will continue to kill, but the ones receiving the ultimate penalty for the ultimate crime will no longer be able to kill!

In the second instance, we should consider the sanctity of life. This simply means that since man has been created in the image of God, there is something holy and sacred about life.

The purpose then of this commandment is the preservation of life. It is to teach us that we are to honor and hold human life in the highest esteem. Created in the image and after the likeness of God, man's life is of infinite worth and value to God. In fact, God demands that human life be valued above all the wealth in the world. Jesus asked, "What is a man profited if he should gain the whole world and lose his soul? Or, what shall a man give in exchange for his soul?" (Matthew 16:26 KJV). Thus, the sanctity of life acknowledges man as God's master creation, his precious possession, his royal masterpiece, and his priceless property.

Observe what is forbidden by this commandment. The King James Version of Exodus 20:13 says, "Thou shalt not kill." The Hebrew word for *kill* is a word that speaks of murder. More specifically, it means premeditated, planned, deliberate, intentional, and unauthorized murder. This word comes from a root that means to "dash to pieces." It describes someone's life being willfully and wrongly taken by the hands of another. It is what we would call murder in the first degree or homicide.

Now scripture does mention some killings that do not fall into the category of murder. Numbers 35 speak of people who were killed accidentally with no malicious intent. God's law provided for the killers a place of asylum, cities of refuge throughout the Promised Land. There they could flee and remain safe from those who wish to avenge loved ones until they could sort out the facts.

Killing in self-defense was allowed, but the use of nonlethal force was particularly emphasized. One should not use lethal force if he or she can avoid doing so. Even if one's home is burglarized during the day, the homeowner is not to use lethal force (Exodus 22:2–3 KJV). Of course, capital punishment in the Old Testament was not considered murder as it was sanctioned for use by the government. God established a legal standard of justice for persons who in fact committed murder. "You shall give life for life" (Exodus 21:23 KJV). The punishment for murder was the death penalty. When one person willfully took the life of another, that individual then had to forfeit his or her life. As New Testament believers, the apostle Paul tells us in Romans 13 that we are obligated to obey the laws of government.

Besides self-defense and capital punishment, war was also not classified as murder, though it involved killing. In scripture, we find God commanding his people to use force in engaging others in war in order to carry out purposes that were just, moral, and defensive approximately thirty times. In fact, for His people to enter the Promised Land, they had to conquer it through warfare.

Hence, this sixth commandment prohibits killing in the form of murder. This was God's way of preserving the sanctity the holiness, and the preciousness of life. Tragically, we see that sanctity being violated in such common practices as abortion, euthanasia, and assisted killing now. Even suicide, the killing of oneself, is prohibited by this commandment. God alone gives life, and he alone is to determine its end.

Finally, beyond the source and the sanctity of life, let us now consider the significance of life. God's law and commandment for the protection of life indicates that he places a great premium and value on life. Of all the commandments that address our relationship with one another, there is much seriousness about violating this sixth commandment (unlike the others). Take the life of another, and that action is irreversible. It is impossible to give back life since death is final, at least in this dispensation.

Hence, we should not murder others, for in doing so, we are terminating the fulfillment of God's purpose in that person's life. While God's purpose includes the salvation of all and he desires none to perish, to murder people before they actually come to Christ is to condemn them to eternal damnation. God's desire is for the preservation of life and the granting of eternal life. During the earthly ministry of Jesus, he contrasted his mission with that of a thief. He said that the thief came only to steal, kill, and destroy but that he had come to bring abundant life (John 10:10 KJV).

It is this offer of abundant life that gives our lives significance. To end it by murder is to deprive one of the experience of loving God and being loved by God. It deprives one of feeling unspeakable joy, glory, and peace that surpasses all human understanding. Murdering others deprives them of a vibrant faith that would allow them to overcome challenges and to even command their mountains to be cast into the sea.

Murder ends all that and more. The murdered are no longer able to represent God in the world as laborers together with him. They are unable to go where he would go and unable to do and act as he would do and act. They are unable to speak and love unconditionally as God would. Not only are the murdered people victimized, but the world at large experiences a great deprivation as a result of their demise.

Hear again the sixth commandment, "Thou shall not kill," and think of murder. God is the source of life. The sanctity of life must always be protected. The significance of life must always be affirmed. In concluding, we ask how might we fulfill this commandment. What is the solution so that we don't kill?

Jesus gives the answer. It really begins in the heart of man. The Lord taught that murder was much deeper than an outward act. He enlarged the meaning to include both the anger that is aroused within the heart and the motives that drive a person to kill. In other words, fix the heart and change the motives, and one will not be driven to kill. Jesus said that we should not become angry with one another since such emotions lead to hatred, bitterness, rage, contempt, dislike, and fury.

The antidote to get rid of anger is to replace it with love—true love, genuine love, godly love. Paul spoke about this kind of love when he wrote the saints at Corinth. It's the kind that suffers long, that is kind, that does not boast or is envious, that does not rejoice in wrongdoing but rejoices in the truth. This kind of love believes all things, hopes all things, and endures all things.

So when you have this kind of love, you desire not to hurt,

harm, wound, or destroy others. In fact, such love drives and compels you to do the following:

> Rescue the perishing, care for the dying;
> Snatch them in pity from sin and the grave
> Weep o'er the erring ones. Lift up the fallen!
> Tell them of Jesus, the mighty to save.[7]

Commandment 6: 10 Questions

1. What is the first recorded murder in scripture? What was God's response?
2. Opponents of capital punishment cite the possibility of the innocent being executed. What is your view, considering the availability of DNA testing and other methods to prove guilt?
3. The effectiveness of the drugs involved in lethal injection and the possibility that they cause unjust suffering have recently been called into question. Is it possible to carry out capital punishment in a *compassionate* way?
4. Opponents of capital punishment cite the capricious manner in which it is carried out, especially what appears to be the "luck of the draw." Can the system be fixed to guard against this reality?
5. Critics of religion cite such *inconsistency* as God commanding his people to kill the inhabitants of the Promised Land in Israel's conquest of that land. How do you explain God's actions to them?
6. Death, regardless of its manner, negates the possibility of making peace with God if such was not done prior. What is your view when capital punishment by the state creates this reality?
7. Assisted suicide has been legalized in some countries. What are your views on this?
8. Some religious groups have extended this commandment to include all animal life, including even insects. Of course, their diet consists entirely of fruits, vegetables, and grain. Did God have this in mind when he issued this sixth commandment?
9. What do you consider the best alternative for capital punishment?
10. Can a murderer ever be rehabilitated?

CHAPTER 8

COMMANDMENT #7: "KEEPING THE MARRIAGE UNDEFILED"
(EXODUS 20:14)

Of all the rites, rituals, and celebrations that take place in the church, weddings rank near the top of the list for me. There is something almost spellbinding when we hear those familiar words: "Dearly beloved, we are gathered here in the sight of God and in the face of this congregation to join together this man and this woman in holy matrimony."

As a minister, I have been involved in numerous weddings. As a father, I have actually been responsible for one. Weddings can be a big deal as evidenced by all the wedding shows that are sponsored each year. At such shows, you are exposed to everything related to weddings, and in fact, you can book such services on the spot.

Weddings are beautiful occasions, especially when the couple adds their personal touch to the ceremony. We still remember that wedding the summer of 2009 when bride Jill Peterson and groom Kevin Heinz led their wedding party down the aisle, dancing to the song "Forever" by Chris Brown. I remember seeing another similar entrance on the television show *Four Weddings*, which ranked the events in several categories. The winning couple received an all-expense paid honeymoon to a tropical island. The black couple in the contest featured the groomsmen coming down the aisle and doing *the worm*. Unfortunately, the other three brides gave that ceremony the absolute lowest score. Sadly, that couple came in last in the overall contest.

Now in spite of the pomp and circumstance as well as the bells and whistles that accompany weddings, weddings are ultimately about the vows a bride and groom pledge to each other as they stand before God and in the presence of God's people. They pledge to love, honor, comfort, and cherish each other. They pledge to do so for better or worse, for richer or poorer, and in sickness and in health. Furthermore, they confirm their pledge by giving and receiving rings.

I wish it was possible that we could now say, "They lived happily ever after!" While many such relationships may have started out well, this relationship likely did not last forever. Indeed, we are told that 50 percent of all marriages end in divorce. Even more alarming, so-called Christian marriages have not been able to escape this reality. The divorce rate in the church is virtually the same as it is in the world.

What accounts for the breakup of so many marriages? Unfortunately, the most frequent reason given is the one that is not easily understood, namely "irreconcilable differences." Some people see this not so much as a reason but as an excuse. You want out of a marriage, and you don't have any real reason that the two of you could not work out, so you call it irreconcilable differences. Now another leading reason for the dissolution of marriages is that of adultery. Adultery means that one engages in sexual relations with someone other than one's spouse.

When man was created, God endowed him with sexual desires. That allowed for man to fulfill God's command to be fruitful and multiply. This sexual desire was to build a close bond between husband and wife and to allow them to populate the earth. While this sexual desire is strong, God knows that for man's own well-being, this desire needs to be controlled and kept in check. Thus, for the marriage bond, man was meant to keep this sexual desire within the marriage. Hence, the command to not commit adultery.

Consider now in the first instance the causes of adultery. While we acknowledge the role of Satan in deceiving man to act contrary to God's will, we must also acknowledge the role that man himself also plays. At the core of man's commitment of adultery is that of selfishness, concern only about him or herself, what the individual feels he or she is entitled to. If the spouse is no longer able to deliver or to live up to those expectations, the result oftentimes is adultery.

Even before the act itself, the tendency is to think and fantasize about that forbidden act. That is what our first parents did in the garden of Eden. God had told them not to eat of the Tree of the Knowledge of Good and Evil, less they surely die. Along came the serpent and told them otherwise. He said that they wouldn't die but that their eyes would now be opened. So they fantasized about eating of that tree and experiencing what the serpent told them even before the actual act of eating. That is what happens in adultery. The mind wanders, and then forbidden acts ensue.

So it is inward desires. It's selfish lusts that result in the act of adultery. Even the attitude that says you can look without touching is rejected by Jesus. He taught that if a man looked at a woman with lust, he has already committed adultery in his heart (Matthew 5:28 KJV). Furthermore, he taught that if your right eye caused you to sin, to pluck it out, and if your right hand caused you to sin, to cut it off (Matthew 5:29–30 KJV). While adultery can be forgiven by God and even by the offended spouse, God yet wants us to strenuously avoid such lusting that could result in the sinful act.

Furthermore, adultery is caused by having unrealistic expectations of our spouses and being unreasonably dissatisfied with them when they cannot deliver. Who of us in our adulthood has maintained our high school's body and weight? Who of us in our adulthood has maintained our energy level, our vim and vigor as in the days of our youth! More than just the physical must sustain all marriages.

Second, beyond the causes of adultery, consider now the consequences of adultery. In God's Word, recorded in Genesis 2:24 KJV and Matthew 19:5 KJV, it speaks of a man leaving his father and mother and cleaving to his wife, becoming one flesh. The word *cleave* means to cling to or adhere to. It describes something being glued or cemented together. The idea is that faithfulness is a must to sustain a marriage.

The National Opinion Research Center reports that roughly 15 percent of married or previously married Americans have committed adultery.[8] Other studies have given even higher numbers! It is not a bad idea for us to hear every now and then the words of the wedding vows, "forsaking all others, keeping thee only unto him or her, as long as you both shall live." The consequences of adultery are grim and dire. Once such an act has been committed, the guilty must resort to living a lie. The individual must lie about his or her time, activities, schedules, whereabouts, and even money. Then also this offense takes away from the dynamics of the guilty party's home life. The other spouse is neglected. Children now seem to be an irritation. There is no sense of joy, peace, and happiness in the home. Because the adulterer has to divide his or her money between home and the affair, the result oftentimes is financial hardship in that household. The rent or mortgage is compromised. Utility, food, and school bills may become delinquent.

Since God intended for sex to be confined to the marriage bond, any violation of the seventh commandment compromises the sexual purity of that marriage. It's always possible that one brings home sexually transmitted diseases, almost dooming the marriage to failure. When the wife is the adulterer, there is also the issue of paternity when children are born. What a sad day we are living in when a television series is devoted to paternity testing, doing it in such a way that brings out the worst in men and women. It is no longer funny when a woman for the tenth time has a man's DNA tested to see if he is the father of her child!

Thus, God says to us, "You shall not commit adultery." The marriage vows says, "Those whom God has joined together, let no man put asunder." Let us pray and act so that by God's grace adultery might not sever the bonds of our marriages.

Finally, let us now consider the cure for adultery. Of course, the starting point is to seek God's forgiveness as well as that of the betrayed spouse. Then let us ask God to give us the conviction to cease from wondering and going astray. As in everything, we need the Lord's help, even to honor our wedding vows. So in the face of temptation, our option is to "ask the Savior to help you; comfort, strengthen and keep you. He is willing to aid you. He will carry you through."

There is yet more that we can do to keep marriage honorable and the bed undefiled. There is something we can do to avoid adultery—an offense so despised by God that its penalty was death by stoning in Old Testament times (Leviticus 20:10). The remedy begins with our avoiding certain things. We are to avoid compromising situations and remove ourselves from the source of temptation. The Bible says we are to flee from sexual immorality (1 Corinthians 6:18 KJV). Running this Christian race means a willingness to run away from certain circumstances.

We should also avoid bad influences. Peer pressure affects not only young people but adults as well. Keep listening to the exploits of others and their boasts of sexual conquests, and soon you may be enticed to follow suit. Paul warned that such sin functions as leaven (yeast) and thus can contaminate our lives, homes, and churches if not removed. The Bible cautions us not to be deceived because bad company corrupts good morals (1 Corinthians 15:33 KJV). Add to these our avoidance of lustful thinking, of bringing every thought into captivity to the obedience of Christ.

The cure for adultery is not only about avoidance of certain things but also about our cultivation of other things. We need to work on developing loving marriages, especially considering the fact that marriage represents the relationship of Christ with his church. We must learn to first do for our spouses and give to them what we would want for ourselves.

Then also let us not forget that the couple that prays together stays together. Rather than ignoring or taking each other for granted, couples should strive to grow together spiritually, hiding God's Word in their hearts so that they might not sin against him. Couples need to pray earnestly, sincerely, and unceasingly, "Lead us not into temptation, but deliver us from evil."

In closing, I offer a tale of two men to illustrate the harm of adultery and conversely the bliss of fidelity. Consider the adulterer, a man after God's own heart by the name of David. His adultery with Bathsheba, which resulted in her pregnancy, was a tragedy. In time David would have her husband, Uriah, killed in battle. But David would also learn that God's children cannot sin without stirring God's wrath. The prophet Nathan told David that the sword would never depart from his house, that he would experience trouble and violence in his home. One son would try to topple him from his throne. The child conceived in adultery would die after just seven days of life. Three of David's sons would be killed by the sword too.

Now the other man, a man named Joseph, models for us how to respond in the face of temptation. He was propositioned by the wife of Potiphar. She even physically grabbed him. Joseph overcame this potential temptation by resolving not to sin against God and then actually fleeing from the presence of Potiphar's wife. While he lost his garment, he maintained his purity. The result was that Joseph would rise to prominence in Egypt, and then the favor of God would come to rest upon his life. Why? Because he yielded not to temptation.

Yes, couples have issues, problems, and challenges, but if they learn how to turn them over to the Lord, He will work them out. If couples learn how to trust and never doubt God, he will surely bring them out. May couples "lean not to their own understanding, but in all their ways acknowledge God, knowing that He will direct their path" (Proverbs 3:5–6 KJV).

Commandment 7: 10 Questions

1. What gender do you think is most guilty of adultery, and why?
2. The penalty for adultery in Old Testament times was death by stoning. What are your views on this practice?
3. Should the government involve itself in the matter of adultery?
4. How did Jesus address the issue of adultery?
5. Recently, an Internet-based organization named Ashley Madison made headlines for its promotion of adulterous affairs. Should such businesses be allowed to exist?
6. This chapter introduced some reasons for adultery. Can you think of any other reasons?
7. Are plural marriages, including group marriages, a viable solution for adultery?
8. Cite an Old Testament example of adultery and the harm it caused.
9. Is adultery a worst offense than fornication? Why, or why not?
10. Is it truly possible to heal following the act of adultery? How?

CHAPTER 9

COMMANDMENT #8: "STOP, THIEF"
(EXODUS 20:15)

Several years ago the world witnessed an unbelievable act of savagery and brutality. The popular ABC *20/20* program presented a broadcast of an actual sentence of amputation carried out in a Middle Eastern country. The offender had committed the crime of theft and was thus subject to what is called Sharia law, which called for the amputation of the perpetrator's arm. While I cannot recall specifically what he had stolen, I do remember it being rather petty, and I reasoned that if the crime had been committed in the United States, the offender may have only been fined and ordered to pay restitution. Thankfully, ABC had the decency to blur the actual hacking of the man's arm, and people only saw the bandaged result.

Fast-forward several years to New York City and an American stockbroker, investment adviser, and financier. That crime of theft did not involve such weapons as knives and guns, and in fact, it was technically committed with computers, pens, and paper. It was called a Ponzi scheme, which resulted in thousands of investors losing billions of dollars. The impact of that crime affected many lives, and it continues to do so. Many elderly people lost the money that was meant to provide for them during their retirement years. The pension funds of many municipalities were adversely affected, putting the financial future of their retirees at risk.

Technically, the crime was securities fraud, and the perpetrator was Bernie Madoff. On June 29, 2009, he was sentenced to 150 years in prison.

No one is immune to theft. By the time we reach adulthood, all of us have been subjected to some theft. In the new millennium, the Bureau of Justice reported that for every one thousand households, 31.8 homes were burglarized. So too, a bank robbery occurred just under every fifty-two minutes, though not always with a gun pointed at a teller's head. Further statistics included 1.2 million car thefts, and the estimated twenty-five-million-dollar loss to retailers as a result of shoplifting and employee theft.[9]

God's eighth commandment cries out to us, "You shall not steal." In looking at this commandment, we will consider the wrong way to get things as well as the right way to get them. Finally, we will consider the rewards we experience from rightfully obtaining things.

First, consider the wrong way to get things, which we call theft or stealing. This is when a person wrongfully takes from another what belongs to the owner. Just as God values the sanctity of life in forbidding us to commit murder, he also values the sanctity of property and thus forbids us to steal. In fact, this eighth commandment is emphasized and reiterated in several places in scripture. In Leviticus 19:11 (KJV), we are told. "You shall not steal, neither deal falsely, neither lie one to another." Deuteronomy 5:19 (KJV) reads, "Neither shall you steal." Then in Ephesians 4:28 (KJV), we are told, "Let him that stole, steal no more."

Stealing then is getting things dishonestly, taking something that is not yours. Now theft is more than just stealing another person's physical property. It could also include the theft of time. So when we clock into the job and do other personal things besides the work we are responsible for, that is theft. It is not uncommon today for workers to get into trouble in the workplace for abusing the use of their computers while on the job. They do so by engaging in chat rooms, online shopping, online gambling, and even online pornography. Let the employer dock them some pay, and chances are they will act out and act up!

The fastest form of theft today is that of identity theft. A few years ago, the *New York Times* reported that about 3.3 million American consumers had their personal information stolen and used to open fraudulent bank, credit cards, or utility accounts. These cases collectively cost businesses $32.9 billion and consumers $3.8 billon. It then took some sixty hours to repair the credit history of the victims.[10]

"Thou shall not steal." This also includes copying or downloading music from the Internet without paying for it. This also includes plagiarism, using someone else's words without attributing them as the source. "Thou shall not steal!" This includes not reporting all of one's income for the purpose of rent calculation in government assisted housing. It includes claiming deductions on tax returns that one has not qualified for. And the list goes on and on. Whatever the temptation to take from others what we have not earned, God says, "Thou shall not steal."

Second, consider now the right way to get things. Hear Paul's admonition in Ephesians 4:28 KJV, "Let him that stole, steal no more: but rather let him labor working with his hands the thing which is good, that he may have to give to him that needeth." Believers in particular are not to steal to acquire wealth and possessions but are to work for it. In scripture we read that work is ordained of God. In the very beginning after he had created Adam and Eve, God placed them in the garden of Eden and gave them the responsibility of tending the land. They truly had to work in order to eat. In the New Testament, the apostle Paul spoke of the example he set in working to provide for himself and others, and he warned that those who did not do so had no right to eat (2 Thessalonians 3:6–12 KJV).

Work then is the antidote for stealing, and it is God's way for us to get things. He endows us with strength and abilities to be gainfully employed in order to provide for ourselves. No wonder scripture describes work as a gift of God "that every man should eat and drink, and enjoy the good of his labor; it is the gift of God" (Ecclesiastes 3:13 KJV).

At the core of stealing is selfishness, coveting and wanting what someone else has but without expending the efforts to gain that thing lawfully. Especially for believers, we must learn how to be content with what God has given us. So what if someone else has more money? To God yet be the glory. So what if someone else has a fancy car and you don't? To God yet be the glory. So what if someone else lives in a modern, state-of-the-art house and you do not? To God yet be the glory. You just prepare yourself as best as you can and then work as hard as you can, and be grateful for whatever the Lord allows you to have and thank Him just the same.

So with whatever we desire to have, may we resist the temptation to steal and instead seek to work hard to get it. Even as we do so, we do so believing that with God all things are possible. He will bless our endeavors and in time allow our efforts to bear fruit.

History bears record of a young girl who had a desire to become great. Sadly, at the age of five, she was diagnosed with polio, and doctors said she would never walk. But with the help of her mother and many siblings, not to mention her own self-discipline, she would overcome her condition. After much therapy, she decided to take off her cumbersome leg brace, and at age twelve she tried walking on her own. Soon she began to run and then to play sports, excelling in track and field. In 1956, she won a bronze medal in the Olympics, and then in 1960, she won three gold medals. That girl was Wilma Rudolph.[11] The point is that we should work for what we desire and not resort to stealing.

Finally, consider the reward we experience when we obtain things the right way rather than resorting to theft. A thief will steal, but the individual cannot rejoice in what he or she has obtained unlawfully. There is always the fear that the thief will eventually be caught and exposed for who he or she really is. On the other hand, if you work hard and earn what you have, you have the right to enjoy it. Work is the legitimate means God has ordained for us to get things in this life.

The virtue of honesty is clearly opposed to stealing. Such virtue God honors in a person by granting the individual his constant presence and care. He watches over these honest folks. He preserves them from all evil. In fact, he makes them to lie down in green pastures. He leads them besides still waters. He restores their souls. He leads them in the path of righteousness for his name's sake so that goodness and mercy follow them all the days of their lives.

So when you're honest in your getting and you have the Lord in your life, the Bible says you are better off than the person with great treasure. Such an honest person earns eternal treasures that are safely stored in heaven, where neither moth nor rust doth corrupt and where thieves do not break through and steal.

May we be encouraged not to steal and hence avoid risking the possibility of not inheriting the kingdom of God, avoid defiling ourselves, and avoid provoking the wrath of God. May we be encouraged not to steal and hence avoid causing harm to others and compromising the well-being of others. May we be encouraged not to steal and hence avoid the possibility of having to pay a greater restitution.

"Thou shall not steal." We are subject to succumb to the temptation to steal. But even in our succumbing, there is yet grace to be realized. When we confess, God will forgive, and then he will convict us to do the right thing by making amends and restitution.

I close this section by calling as a witness one by the name of Zacchaeus, a reformed and transformed thief. He now has become a new creature in Christ, experiencing the passing away of old things and beholding all things becoming new. Zacchaeus was the chief among the publicans, and he was rich. He made his fortune from extorting taxes from those least able to afford them. God gave him the conviction and desire to see Christ. Being of small stature, he climbed a tree just to get a glimpse of the Master. Jesus looked up and saw him and then told the man to come down so that he might abide at Zacchaeus's house that very same day. The Bible says that Zacchaeus made haste coming down and receiving Jesus joyfully. That very moment he was saved and given a new name that was written down in glory. Now saved, Zacchaeus wanted to evidence the change in his life. Once he was a thief, but now he was a man of honesty. Now saved, he pledged to right the wrongs he had done, offering to give half of his possessions to the poor.

What a model of the Lord's saving grace and his transforming power. The once thief is now an honest man. That is what the Lord's amazing grace will do. The lost can be found. The blind can be given sight. Those in bondage can be set free. Though your sins be as scarlet, he can wash you white as snow. When he does, make certain you serve him. When he does, make certain that you follow him. When he does, make certain to exalt his name. When he does, then tell of his goodness. When he does, "lift Him up by living, as a Christian ought; let the world in you the Savior see. Then men, will gladly follow Him, who once taught, I'll draw all men unto me."

Commandment 8: 10 Questions

1. Joshua 7:21 records the first sin committed by Israel after entering the Promised Land. Achan stole the spoils of war. What were the consequences for this act?
2. Acts 5 recounts the actions of Ananias and Sapphira, who were accused of lying to God. They both were punished with death. How would you have handled their offense?
3. What are your thoughts on the very common practice of sampling certain fruit (grapes, cherries, etc.) in making purchases at the grocery store?
4. What other commandment violation result in the act of theft?
5. Malachi says that we rob God in the withholding of our tithes (Malachi 3:7–8) and offerings. What are your thoughts regarding this charge?
6. Do you think the Old Testament practice of "restitution several fold" should be the only form of punishment for theft? See Exodus 22:1, 7, 12.
7. Many times in the breakup of a relationship, the charge is made that someone *stole* someone else's spouse, boyfriend, or girlfriend. Is it possible to *steal* someone in this scenario?
8. Proverbs 15:16 talks about a person who fears the Lord being better than one having great treasure. In what way is this true? Did Jesus have anything to say on this matter?
9. Satan is described in scripture as a thief (John 10:10). What does he steal, and what are the consequences?
10. What single virtue do you think is the ultimate antidote for stealing?

CHAPTER 10

COMMANDMENT #9: "SPEAK THE TRUTH, THE WHOLE TRUTH, AND NOTHING BUT THE TRUTH"
(EXODUS 20:16)

The words of this subject are words that are spoken in a court of law as a person prepares to give their testimony on the matter being tried. If one discovers that the witness has lied, the person is guilty of the crime of perjury and subject to possible jail time. Lying has been around since the dawn of human history. The first recorded lie in scripture was that given by the Father of Lies, Satan himself. Appearing in the garden of Eden as a serpent, he contradicted what God had said earlier. Satan told Eve that if she did eat of the forbidden tree, she would not die as God said she would. In time man would come to perfect and master the art of lying!

Nowadays man lies to everyone and lies about everything. In our attempt to sanitize our lying, we oftentimes label them "white lies" or "small fibs." Some of our more common lies include people saying, "You can trust me," "The check is in the mail," "I'm late because I was stuck in traffic," "I just need a couple minutes of your time," or as our parents were fond of saying, "This will hurt me more than it hurts you!" What child being whipped ever believed that one!

We should thank our lucky stars that we are not like the fictional character Pinocchio, whose nose became longer whenever he lied. Can you imagine what we would look like if we, too, experienced the same effect? I wonder how long the nose of someone we assumed was truthful would actually be!

Lest you be tickled by this illustration, understand that lying is no playful joke. Indeed, the consequences can be fatal. You may recall that on January 1, 2000, Governor George H. Ryan suspended all executions in the state of Illinois because evidence had surfaced about how that at least twelve inmates on death row had been falsely accused by the police. In other words, the police who had been sworn to uphold the law had actually broken it by lying about these inmates. As one who accepts the Bible endorsement of capital punishment, I shudder to think about the fate of those inmates in Illinois, some coming within weeks of bidding farewell to this world—all because of the lies of some police.

So the ninth commandment says we are not to bear false witness against our neighbor. We are not to lie to them or lie about them. In examining this commandment, let us consider in the first instance words we should not say to and/or about our neighbors. Second, we will consider the harm such words cause. Finally, we will consider better words. Such lying words deceive others. They are not the truth. Such words may be an exaggeration, a fabrication, or a distortion of the truth. For some people it is just a way of life. No one can trust them. They will lie at the drop of a hat.

In the book *The Day America Told the Truth* by James Patterson, it is reported that 91 percent of people who were surveyed lie routinely about matters they consider trivial, and 36 percent lie about important matters. Then 86 percent lied regularly to parents, 75 percent to friends, 73 percent to siblings, and 69 percent to spouses. Such proves that lying in our culture is an epidemic. God says it should not happen.

Besides lying words, we should not speak gossip against our neighbor. Gossip is anything said about another person that should not be spoken. What is said may be true or just rumor, but it has the potential to harm the other person's reputation. Scripture refers to a gossiper as a "whisperer" who ruins friendships (Proverbs 16:28 KJV) and a "talebearer" who can't be trusted. It is a small person who lacks confidence in themselves who engages in gossip. They believe that by tearing someone apart, they are building up themselves, but nothing could be further from the truth.

Not even the clergy are exempted from gossip, for such was the experience of a new pastor just one month into his pastorate. The rumor was that he had taken his wife to a concert after prayer meeting, fussed at her as they sat in the front row, then made a scene as they left, marching her down the aisle before the concert was over.

He let the rumor circulate for a few weeks and then addressed it. He told the congregation that the story was not true for four reasons. First, he would not take any woman to a concert after prayer meeting. Second, he would not argue with any woman in public. Third, he would not create a scene while any event was taking place. That would deprive others of their right to enjoyment. Fourth and most importantly, he said, "I am not even married!"

So we are not to speak lying and gossiping words to and about our neighbors. So too, we are not to speak words that slander our neighbor. Slander is speaking damaging words with the intent to harm another. God calls this "giving your mouth to evil" as you speak against someone, even those very close to you (Psalm 50:19–20 KJV). It is also known as backbiting. Some of you may recall some years ago the popular group The O'Jays cautioning you against such people. These people smiled to your face but all the time wanted to take your place. So with the help of the almighty God, try not to speak lying words, gossip, or slanderous words against your neighbor, for God will hold you guilty.

Consider now in the second instance the harm such words cause. We used to have a saying when I was young. "Sticks and stones may break my bones, but words can never hurt me." Truth is that words do hurt and harm. Reputations have been destroyed because of lying, gossiping, and slandering. Characters have been ruined. Relationships and friendships have been severed because of lies, gossip, and slander. People have experienced tremendous loses because of these. No wonder scripture says that God hates lying lips (Proverbs 12:22 KJV).

In the book titled *Ten Rules For Living*, Clovis Chappell writes, "There is no measuring the pain, the heartache and the tears that the bearing of false witness has caused. Such a man robs his victim of treasures that are more priceless than life." As is commonly known, the tongue is one of the smallest body parts, yet the Bible says of it, "No man can tame it; it is an unruly evil, full of deadly poison" (James 3:8 KJV).

It is this destructive weapon that devises mischief and works deceitfully. Its harm can rarely be undone. It is this destructive weapon that has killed many good names and reputations. Our challenge and encouragement is to resist the temptation to speak such words. Even in the face of temptation, *zip it* if you have to! Only then will you have no regrets. That way you did not say something you later wished you could take back. Only then would you not have to apologize. You would have held your peace.

Finally, in opposition to words that lie, gossip, and slander, I want to propose some better words we might use toward our neighbor. May we speak words of encouragement, instilling hope and confidence in others. The Bible calls it "provoking one another to love and good works."

Hence, an encouraging word will give hope to those in despair, will stimulate the faith of those in doubt, and will prompt those about to give up to keep going. Such words that encourage will help the uncertain become convinced that with Christ they can do all things.

If we have to say something, may we speak words that commend and praise. Such are positive words, life-affirming words, and words that make others feel good about themselves. Let us then tell them how beautiful they are, how wonderful they are, how nice and gracious they are, how smart and intelligent they are, how useful and helpful they are. The list goes on and on.

Now if by chance we struggle to say anything good about our neighbors, there is something positive we can say on their behalf. We can speak words of prayer on their behalf, asking God to work in their lives and to use them to his honor and glory. Let us pray for God to bless them, to prosper them, to heal them, to deliver them, and to open doors for them.

As we lift them up in prayer, we do so with the conviction that "the fervent, effectual prayer of the righteous availeth much" (James 5:16 KJV). We lift them up in prayer, believing that we shall receive those things we desire when we ask. As for me, I would rather pray for others than lie about them, gossip about them, or slander their names.

Hear again this ninth commandment, "Thou shall not bear false witness against thy neighbor." Such conduct is contrary to the very nature of God, who is a God of truth. Scripture declares, "God is not a man, that He should lie" (Numbers 23:19 KJV). The writer of Deuteronomy wrote, "He is a God of truth and without iniquity, just and right is He" (Deuteronomy 32:4 KJV). Paul wrote to Titus, his son in the ministry, testifying that God cannot lie (Titus 1:2 KVJ). Finally, the writer of Hebrews wrote that it was impossible for God to lie (Hebrew 6:18 KJV).

I urge you now not to bear false witness against your neighbor. Instead, always speak the truth in love to them. If you are consistently lying, you run the risk of not inheriting the kingdom God. Instead you may be sentenced to eternity in that awful place called hell. If you are consistently bearing false witness, you forfeit the favor of God and instead invite and attract the attention of Satan in your life.

Scripture admonishes the believer to put away lying and urges every man to speak the truth (Ephesians 4:25 KJV). The starting point is in our minds and our hearts. Hence, we are exhorted to think on things that are true, honest, just, pure, lovely, and of good report.

Be inspired to imitate Jesus as he went head-to-head with the devil in the wilderness, appealing to the Word of God. Hide God's Word in your heart so that you might not sin against him. Allow God's Word to be a lamp unto your feet and a light unto your path. Allow his Word to be your light in the darkness of this age.

God's Word will cleanse a young man's ways. God's Word will purify your soul such that you love others fervently with a pure heart. When you allow the Word of God to dwell in you rather than lie, gossip, or slander, you will then teach and admonish one another in psalms and hymns and spiritual songs. Now if you are still struggling with what you ought to say to others, especially in the face of temptation, declare, "May the words of my mouth and the meditation of my heart be acceptable in they sight, O Lord my strength and my redeemer" (Psalm 19:14 KJV).

Commandment 9: 10 Questions

1. Proverbs 6:16–19 lists lying as an abomination to the Lord. What do you think makes it such?
2. Is it right to *rank* the sin of lying according to white lies versus deceptive lies?
3. Some Christian leaders are prone to *exaggerate* facts as in church membership numbers, or they suggest they have studied at certain schools when they may have only attended a meeting or a session there. How should the church deal with such exaggeration?
4. Our present times have seen an escalation in religious persecution, especially among Christians. Self-identifying as Christian has brought death in many instances. Is it ever *right* to tell a lie, even for the sake of self-preservation?
5. Possibly one of the biggest areas of lying is not reporting all income when filing tax returns. Is this ever justified?
6. Cite some ways in which lying is harmful to others.
7. What are steps a believer can take to deal with the sin of lying?
8. Scripture calls Satan the Father of Lies and God as the source of truth. Cite examples of the differences in the characters of the two.
9. What are some scriptural consequences for liars?
10. What are some benefits of keeping this ninth commandment?

CHAPTER 11

COMMANDMENT #10: "GIVE ME MORE"
(EXODUS 20:17)

There is a story about a poor peasant who grumbled to a wealthy landlord about the unfairness of it all. He had virtually nothing, and it seemed that the landlord had it all. Knowing the greedy nature of man, the landlord promised to give the peasant all the land he could walk around in a whole day. The offer just seemed so unbelievable to the peasant, but he acted on it just the same. He began walking, circling as large an area as he could. He wanted to capitalize on such an opportunity that he ended up overexerting himself and dropping dead from a heart attack. In his quest to get more, he ended up with nothing, save death!

"Give me more" is the prevalent mind-set in this day and age. There is a widespread dissatisfaction with what we now have and an insatiable craving for more, even more than we actually need. The Bible has a word for this, and it is called *covetousness*. Hence, this tenth commandment, "Thou shalt not covet."

Interestingly, the apostle Paul wrote that in "the last days perilous times will come" and one of the marks of such time is men being "lovers of their own selves, covetous, boasters, proud, blasphemers, disobedient to parents, unthankful, unholy" (2 Timothy 3:1 NKJV).

This word *covet* simply means to delight in something. It describes a strong desire to possess something, and the word is often translated as *lust*. It depicts an excessive desire for something.

While the thing in and of itself may not be bad, the excessive craving for it makes it bad for us.

The unfortunate reality that confronts us today is that we are bombarded with media that tells us we need more! This is reflected in television programming and advertisements. Not too long ago there was a television series titled *Lifestyles of the Rich and Famous*. We were shown their homes, their yachts, their designer clothing, their priceless paintings, their fancy vacations in remote places around the world, and the list goes on and on. All of this was designed to stir up our lust for more things and to convince us that somehow we were not truly fulfilled unless we had these things. And so this tenth commandment says to us, "Thou shalt not covet."

In examining this commandment, we shall consider in the first instance the prohibition that is mandated. In the second instance, we will examine the exception that is encouraged. Finally, we will consider the stipulation offered.

First, note the prohibition that is mandated. "Thou shalt not covet." The categories are next listed—our neighbors' houses, spouses, servants, and even animals. In an agricultural society where wealth was measured by the size of one's herd and one's household, these specific prohibitions were relevant. In short, for us today we are not to covet anything that belongs to our neighbor.

It is said that covetousness is the mother of all sins since all the other nine commandments are rooted in this particular sin, especially the commandments about dealing with man's relationship with others. These commandments in particular deal with outward behavior—honoring parents, not killing, not stealing, not committing adultery, and not lying. This tenth commandment deals with one's mind-set, the attitude of one's heart. If we can just control our passion to not covet and to not excessively desire what belongs to others, chances are we will honor parents, not kill, not steal, not commit adultery, and not lie. Indeed, we will be more inclined to respect others and to acknowledge their sanctity and holiness. Not coveting prompts us to honor the sanctity of family, people, and property.

So in this tenth commandment, the focus goes beyond our outward behavior and probes at the level of our internal attitudes where sin begins. It shows that God looks at our hearts, and he desires that we have pure motivations. Truth is that covetousness in people will never be satisfied as there is always more to desire. The Bible speaks of such people and says that their foolish and harmful lusts will result in their being drowned in destruction and perdition, which means hell (1 Timothy 6:9 KJV). Paul wrote that such people will be excluded from heaven (1 Corinthian 6:9–10 KJV).

So God prohibits covetousness in that such people are overly concerned with material things. They are concerned about putting material gain before God rather than seeking first his kingdom and righteousness. Jesus cautioned against such, reasoning that a man's life does not consist in the abundance of things possessed. Furthermore, he questioned the value of covetousness, asking, "What shall it profit a man if he shall gain the whole world, and lose his own soul?" (Mark 8:36 KJV).

"Thou shalt not covet," God says. When you do so, that opens the door to sin. You may not honor your parents. You may not provide for their welfare because you reason that you only have enough for yourself. When we covet, it opens the door to other sins, such as lying, stealing, and even adultery.

There is a huge price tag for the commission of this sin. Angels were booted out of heaven with Lucifer because they wanted to usurp the place of God on his throne. Adam and Eve were booted out of the garden of Eden because they succumbed to the wiles of the devil in the form of the serpent. They were convinced to partake of the forbidden tree. They thought their eyes would be opened and they would become as gods. The people of ancient Judah lost their nation for some seventy years because of their desire to be just like the surrounding nations. To them and to us, God says, "Thou shall not covet."

In the second instance, consider the exception that is encouraged. By this I mean that scripture does make allowance for a certain type of coveting! Paul addressed two such exceptions when he wrote to the church at Corinth. When the issue of speaking in tongues threatened to wreck the church, he advised that rather than emphasizing the gift of tongues, there was a better gift the members were to covet, and that was *prophesying* (1 Corinthians 14:39 KJV).

The usage of that word in the New Testament is commonly meant to proclaim or to preach. Thus, Paul was actually encouraging the members to excessively desire to preach the gospel of Jesus Christ. Nothing was wrong in doing so, and in fact, it was the right thing to do.

Now if there is something commendable to be excessive about, it is proclaiming God's Word and declaring the unsearchable riches of Christ Jesus. Be excessive in letting a dying world know there is a living Christ who came into the world, not to condemn the world but to save the world through his sacrifice (John 3:17). Be excessive in proclaiming, "If any man be in Christ, he is a new creature: old things are passed away; behold, all things are become new" (1 Corinthians 5:17 KJV).

In addition to coveting prophesy, Paul advised the church to covet earnestly the best gifts, and then he showed them a more excellent way, specifically the gift of love (1 Corinthians 13). What better people we would be if we coveted earnestly the gift of love. We would be a better church and indeed a better world.

Now Paul emphasized a particular way of love, what we call agape or godly love. This kind of love is patient and kind. It does not envy or boast. It is not arrogant or rude. It does not insist on its own way. It is not irritable or resentful. This kind of love does not rejoice at wrongdoing but rejoices with the truth. It bears all things, believes all things, hopes all things, and endures all things.

Through the years songwriters and lyricists have reminded us that "what the world needs now is love, sweet love. It's the only thing that there's just too little of." Our challenge is to always be mindful and consider the necessity, the importance, and the urgency of love. Believers have been commanded to love, and that is the evidence of our belonging to Christ. Indeed, we are to emulate the character of God, whom scripture defines as love (1 John 4:8 KJV).

So be excessive in your desire to love all. Do so not only in words but in deeds as well, helping others, encouraging others, inspiring others, and praying for others.

Finally, this tenth commandment calls us to consider the stipulation. By this I mean that scripture makes provision for us to replace covetousness with contentment. Paul wrote about learning to be content in whatever state he found himself in (Philippians 4:11 KJV). His sense of joy, satisfaction, and fulfillment were not based on his material possessions or even his earthly circumstances but simply on the presence of Christ in his life.

Paul's discovery was that true wealth came from being satisfied with God's provisions for his life. He learned satisfaction from that which God provided for him. It may not have been as much as what others had, but he was satisfied. It may not have been as impressive as what others had, but he was still satisfied.

Thus, we are to learn from him. We can still have contentment even if we don't live in a fine house, drive a fine car, or wear fine jewelry and clothing. As long as Christ is in your life, you are infinitely blessed. Such experience enables you to say with conviction, "The world didn't give to me this joy, and the world can't take it away."

We also replace covetousness with contentment by standing on the promises of God. He has promised to provide all of our needs according to his riches in glory. He has promised to never leave us or forsake us. He has promised to grant us those things we desire when we ask. We believe that when we ask, we receive; when we seek, we find; and when we knock, doors will be opened.

May we remember that God is not slack concerning his promises. Our challenge is to trust him. In doing so, we will be blessed because we "tasted him and saw that He is good!"

Furthermore, we replace covetousness with contentment by our reliance on the power of Christ. In and of ourselves, we are unable to resist the pull and attraction of envy, jealousy, and greed. But when we understand the power at our disposal because of the presence of Christ within, we recognize that "we can do all things through Christ who strengthens us" (Philippians 4:13 KJV).

May we all rely on that strength so that we resist the temptation to covet. May we instead pray for others, though many may have more than we do. May we pray that God will bless them even more, realizing that his blessings are inexhaustible. In God's time, he will even take care of us.

"Thou shalt not covet." God has issued his warning, and the consequence for a violation is severe. Ask Achan in the Old Testament, a soldier in the army of Israel. Israel had just experienced a tremendous victory over Jericho, and God had forbidden them to take any of the accursed things of that city. Regrettably, those things were just too enticing for Achan, and he subsequently stole some, resulting in God's wrath poured out against them. When it was over, thirty-six fellow soldiers had died, and Achan and his family were executed.

Covetousness will get you into trouble. Just ask David. One day during his idleness, he saw Bathsheba bathing on her roof. She was just too irresistible for him. He was covetous of the man and the marriage she was already in, and so David committed adultery with her. Then he had her husband killed on the battlefield. Now God was not oblivious to his transgressions. All of this started when he coveted what was not his. In time the child conceived by that illicit union would die after living but a week. David would then experience all kinds of trouble in his household—a daughter raped, a son trying to overthrow him from his throne, and then the violent deaths of some of his sons.

May we also learn our lesson. In the face of temptation, may we call upon that name which is above every name. So what if others crave more, others seek more, others hunger and lust for more? May we "yield not to temptation, for yielding is sin." May we become convicted that "each victory will help you, some other to win." And then may we "fight manfully onward, dark passions subdue," all the while looking ever to Jesus, knowing that "He'll carry you through."

Here's the secret to resisting covetousness. "Ask the Savior to help you, comfort, strengthen, and keep you. He's willing to aid you. He will carry you through."

Commandment 10: 10 Questions

1. What two other commandments did David break as a result of his sin of coveting?
2. Why is covetousness such an ignored sin?
3. First Kings 21 tells the story of King Ahab's coveting of Nabath's vineyard and how he eventually got it. What was the punishment for this crime? Was it fair or right?
4. The previous questions hint at the issue of eminent *domain*. How might covetousness factor into such as issue?
5. There is a television series called *Buried Alive*. It addresses the serious matter of hoarding. What is the relationship between hoarding and covetousness?
6. Is asceticism a viable option to covetousness?
7. What admonition does Paul give to ministers who might be tempted to covet?
8. What are ways we can defeat the sin of covetousness?
9. Many professional athletes have had expensive sneakers produced bearing their names. Almost always they have been manufactured in third world countries for pennies. Is there a correlation between exploitation and covetousness?
10. Note Jesus's teaching in Luke 12:15 regarding possessions. How might a Christian billionaire understand this teaching?

A FINAL WORD

When Pat Robertson released his book on the Ten Commandments in 2004, he titled it *The Ten Offenses*. This was his way of acknowledging how the American culture has drifted away from its historic Judeo-Christian values. He notes how the Founding Fathers of the country were guided by the truth of the Bible and how the laws of the land are rooted in the Ten Commandments of the Old Testament and the Sermon on the Mount of the New Testament.

A little more than a decade after his book's release, something more insidious is taking place. We are witnessing a more brazen affront to God's Word in the United States. This is especially so with our redefinition of marriage and family. Indeed, the nuclear family, consisting of husband/father, wife/mother, and children, long the bedrock of civilization, is now considered the anomaly and is fodder for jokes by late-night comedians.

We now see the president of the United States of America and the first lady congratulating men who make their sexuality public. It seems now that every major corporation promotes its version of family life, always to the exclusion of one gender. Common sense has apparently been abandoned in favor of political correctness. If it takes the biological contribution of a male and a female to create a life, it stands to reason that that new life is best served by the nurture of both male and female.

Perhaps worst of all is the issue of gender dysphoria,

championed by the likes of Caitlyn Jenner, the former Bruce Jenner. How could a man who contributed sperms in impregnating a woman become a woman himself! Have his chromosomes changed? What if he stopped taking artificial hormones? Add to this massive confusion that a person needs to be accepted for whatever he or she identifies as. Not very long ago, the residents of Houston defeated what is commonly called the "bathroom bill." In short, it would have allowed Big Bubba, who is six feet three inches tall and weighs three hundred pounds, a person who also sired eight children by eight different mothers, to use the women's restroom by simply self-identifying as a female! Can you imagine the danger of Big Bubba exposing himself to a little seven-year-old girl in the restroom!

The prophet Isaiah and the apostle Paul both questioned, "Whose report the people would believe?" (Isaiah 55:1; Romans 10:16). Our times urgently call for the people of God to believe his report and to act on that report. This is not to suggest that we attempt to force our beliefs on others. It does require that we be just as diligent in our witness for God as the world is in rejecting him. Our motivation at all times must be the witness of scripture. "There is a way that seems right to a man, but its end is the way of death" (Proverbs 14:12 KJV). May we do all that we can to counter our times again becoming reminiscent of ancient Israel. "In those days there was no king in Israel; everyone did what was right in his own eyes" (Judges 21:25 KJV).

The faith community is encouraged to again practice the Ten Commandments in our daily living. The Lord's report can only lead to a better world.

NOTES

1. Jennie Wilson, "Hold to God's Unchanging Hand," *The New National Baptist Hymnal* (Nashville: National Baptist Publishing Board, 1977), 248.
2. Lehman Strauss taught Old Testament history at Philadelphia Bible Institute and served as pastor of the Calvary Baptist Church in Bristol, Pennsylvania, from 1939 to 1957.
3. Kenneth W. Osbeck, cited in *Amazing Grace* (Grand Rapids, MI: Kregel Publications, 1990), 348
4. Passage from the *Orderly Book of the Army* under command of Washington, dated at headquarters in the city of New York, August 3, 1770. Reported in American Masonic Register and Literary Companion, volume 1, 1829.
5. Popular song based on Proverbs 18:10.
6. Rohr, Richard. "Resurrected Living," some collected quotes on worship. Posted June 11, 2013.
7. Fannie Crosby, "Rescue the Perishing," *The New National Baptist Hymnal* (Nashville: National Baptist Publishing Board, 1977), 142.
8. Family Research Council (Washington Watch, October 29, 1993), 2. Cited by Higher Praise.com, accessed August 2, 2017.
9. "Crime in the United States 2000" (US Department of Justice, Federal Bureau of Investigation, October 22, 2001)
10. The Associated Press, "Minnesota: Personal Data Is Stolen; 3.3. Million People Are Affected," *New York Times* (March 26, 2010).
11. "Wilma Rudolph," Wikipedia, November 8, 2016.

BIBLIOGRAPHY

Barclay, William. *The Ten Commandments for Today*. Louisville: Westminster John Knox Press, 1998.

Briscoe, D. Stuart. *The Ten Commandments: God's Rules for Living*. Colorado Springs, CO: Water Brook Press, 1995.

Calvin, John. *Sermons on the Ten Commandments*. Grand Rapids, MI: Baker, 1980.

Holbert, John C. *The Ten Commandments*. Nashville: Abingdon Press, 2002.

Hybels, Bill. *Engraved on Your Heart: Living the Ten Commandments Day By Day*. Colorado Springs, CO: Cook Communications Ministries, 2000.

Leadership Ministries Worldwide. *What the Bible Says about the Ten Commandments*. Chattanooga, TN: Alpha-Omega Ministries, Inc., 1997.

Marrs, Ross W. *Be My People: Sermons on the Ten Commandments*; Nashville: Abingdon Press, 1991.

Martin, Glen S. *God's Top Ten List: The Ten Commandments*. Chicago: Moody Press, 1999.

Mitchell, Mark. *Ten*: *How the Commandments Set Us Free*. Grand Rapids, MI: Discovery House, 2016.

Morgan, G. Campbell. *The Ten Commandments*. Eugene, OR: Wipf and Stock Publishers, 1998.

Robertson, Pat. *The Ten Offenses*: *Reclaim the Blessings of the Ten Commandments*. Nashville: Integrity Publishers, 2004.

Stables, Jim. *A Journey through the 10 Commandments*. Lima, OH: Fairway Press, 1991.

Vines, Jerry. *Basic Bible Sermons on the Ten Commandments*. Nashville: Broadman Press, 1992.

West, Robert M. *The Ten Commandments Then and Now*. Uhrichsville, OH: Barbour Publishing, 2010.